Fragile Democracy

FRAGILE
DEMOCRACY
THE STRUGGLE OVER RACE AND VOTING RIGHTS IN NORTH CAROLINA

JAMES L. LELOUDIS & ROBERT R. KORSTAD

THE UNIVERSITY OF NORTH CAROLINA PRESS

Chapel Hill

Publication of this book was supported in part by a generous gift from MARY LOU *and* JIM BABB.

The University of North Carolina Press has been a member of the Green Press Initiative since 2003.

Cover illustration: Mountain Moral Monday protest in Asheville, North Carolina. Courtesy Wikimedia Commons.

Library of Congress Cataloging-in-Publication Data
Names: Leloudis, James L., author. | Korstad, Robert Rodgers, author.
Title: Fragile democracy : the struggle over race and voting rights in North Carolina / James L. Leloudis and Robert R. Korstad.
Description: Chapel Hill : The University of North Carolina Press, 2020. | Includes bibliographical references and index.
Identifiers: LCCN 2020015370 | ISBN 9781469660394 (cloth : alk. paper) | ISBN 9781469661391 (paperback : alk. paper) | ISBN 9781469660400 (ebook)
Subjects: LCSH: African Americans—Suffrage—North Carolina. | Suffrage—North Carolina. | North Carolina—Politics and government—1865–1950. | North Carolina—Politics and government—1951- | North Carolina—Race relations.
Classification: LCC JK1929.N8 L45 2020 | DDC 324.6/2089960730756—dc23
LC record available at https://lccn.loc.gov/2020015370

For generations

of North Carolinians

who held America

accountable to its

democratic aspirations

Contents

Illustrations

MAPS

Fragile Democracy

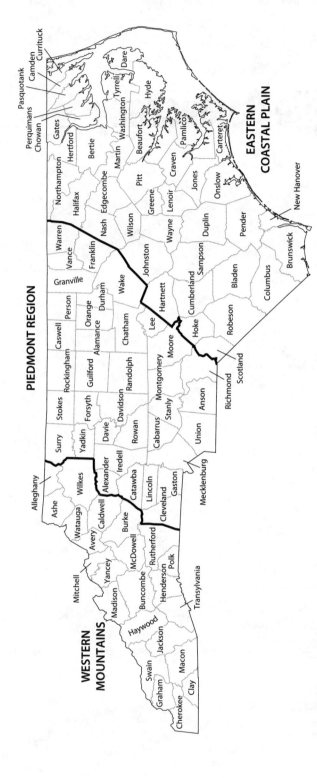

North Carolina regions and counties

North Carolina towns and cities referenced in text

Introduction

America is at war with itself over the right to vote, or, more precisely, over the question of who gets to exercise that right and under what circumstances. Conservatives speak in ominous tones of "America the vulnerable," warning that voter fraud has become so widespread that it threatens public trust in elected government. They insist that lawmakers act at once to reverse the damage by policing voter registration more vigorously and implementing new security measures such as photo ID requirements for access to the ballot box. Progressives counter that electoral fraud is exceedingly rare and that when voting irregularities do occur, they usually involve mistakes made by election officials rather than individual voters' wrongdoing. From this perspective, efforts to change the ways we govern elections are, at best, "a solution in search of a problem." At worst, they constitute a thinly veiled campaign to shrink the electorate and restrict some citizens' right to cast a free and fair ballot.[1]

Over the last decade, North Carolina has been a battleground for this debate. In 2010, riding a tide of voter discontent, Republicans gained control of both houses of North Carolina's General Assembly. The completion of the decennial census in the same year gave them the opportunity to redraw legislative districts in ways that produced a Republican supermajority in the next election. Then, in 2013, the U.S. Supreme Court, ruling in the landmark *Shelby County v. Holder* case, struck down section 5 of the 1965 Voting Rights Act. That section required federal approval of changes to election law in jurisdictions with a history of racial discrimination. It was critical to protecting the voting rights of minority citizens; in its absence, states had an opening to reintroduce discriminatory policies like those that the Voting Rights Act had been meant to abolish. Within a month of the *Shelby* decision, Republican lawmakers in North Carolina took advantage of that opportunity. They passed House Bill (HB) 589, the nation's most comprehensive revision of election law. The legislation required that voters provide photo ID at the polls, shortened the period for early voting, and ended same-day voter registration and out-of-precinct voting—all of which had a dispro-portionate impact on minority, low-income, and elderly electors.

Opposition to these changes was vocal and well organized. It found voice through what came to be known as the Moral Monday move-ment, named for the weekly gatherings of protestors at the legislative building in Raleigh. Reverend William J. Barber II, a charismatic Pen-tecostal minister from Goldsboro and president of the North Carolina Conference of the NAACP, spearheaded the movement. For nearly a de-cade, he had led the North Carolina People's Assembly, an ecumenical and multiracial coalition of organizations that pressured lawmakers— Democrats as well as Republicans—to act on a variety of social welfare issues, from affordable housing and a living wage to criminal justice re-form and improvements in health care and education. The Moral Mon-day movement brought tens of thousands of new participants to this campaign. They marched in Raleigh and in cities across the state to ex-press their opposition to HB 589 and the Republican legislature's policy agenda, which included budget cuts for public education, stricter limits on unemployment benefits, elimination of the state's Earned Income Tax Credit for low-wage workers, refusal of federal funds for Medicaid expansion, and reversal of death penalty reform.

While protestors gathered in the streets and filled the halls of the legislature, attorneys representing the state conference of the NAACP, the American Civil Liberties Union, the League of Women Voters, and the U.S. Department of Justice challenged HB 589 in court. They ar-gued that if left to stand, the law would "cause the denial, dilution, and abridgement of African-Americans' fundamental right to vote"— an effect that would, in turn, discount the voices of other citizens who allied themselves with black voters on issues of public policy. Progres-sives maintained that democracy itself was at stake in the battle over HB 589.[2]

As historians and as participants in these events, we share another observer's sense "that the politics of today is continuous with the past that made it, marked by struggles that have never really ended, only ebbed, shifted, and returned." To understand the issues at stake in today's battle over the ballot box, we must look back to 1865 and the end of the Civil War. The Union had been preserved and the Confeder-acy was in ashes, but the sacrifice of nearly three-quarters of a million lives had not decided the republic's future. Would there be a "new birth of freedom," as Republican president Abraham Lincoln had imagined in his Gettysburg Address, or would the nation be reconstituted as a "white man's government," the outcome championed by his successor, Democrat Andrew Johnson? Between 1865 and 1870, Lincoln's party answered that question with three constitutional amendments that historian Eric Foner has described as America's "Second Founding."[3]

The Thirteenth Amendment (1865) abolished slavery and guaranteed the liberty of four million black men, women, and children who had been enslaved in the South. The Fourteenth (1868) granted them citizenship by birthright and established the principle of "equal protection of the laws." And the Fifteenth (1870) forbade the states from denying or abridging male citizens' right to vote "on account of race, color, or previous condition of servitude."

These constitutional guarantees tied the fate of American democracy to the citizenship rights of a newly emancipated black minority and their descendants. For 150 years, the exercise of those rights and the connection between racial justice and democratic governance have been defining issues in American politics. This has been particularly true of the right to vote.

In North Carolina and the nation, battles over the franchise have played out through cycles of emancipatory politics and conservative retrenchment. In a pattern repeated multiple times, blacks and their allies have formed political movements to end racial discrimination and claim their rights as equal citizens. They have done so not only to advance their own interests but also to promote participatory democracy more generally and to make government responsive to the needs of all its people. Invariably, conservative white lawmakers have countered such efforts by erecting barriers around the ballot box. They have been remarkably creative in that work. When one restriction was struck down in the courts or through protest and political mobilization, they quickly invented another. Sometimes they justified their actions in overtly racial terms and implemented reforms through violent means. At other times they spoke euphemistically of fraud and corruption. Always, they presented strict regulation of the right to vote as a means of ensuring "good order" and "good government."[4]

Some pundits have suggested that the fight over ballots represents little more than competition between Democrats and Republicans to reshape the electorate and gain partisan advantage. No doubt the contest has been intensely partisan, but the ideological realignment of the Democratic and Republican parties in North Carolina reminds us that something far more significant has been at stake. In the decades immediately after the Civil War, conservatives called themselves Democrats, campaigned against government policies that redressed inequality, and conspired to deny black men the right to vote, while Republicans identified as social progressives, championed a more expansive and generous state, and fought for universal male suffrage. Beginning in the mid-twentieth century, these positions flipped. Grassroots activists and national leaders reshaped the Democratic Party to support the advancement of civil rights, and Republicans aligned themselves as advocates for small government, limited federal involvement in state and local affairs, and a restrictive stance toward citizenship and its attendant rights.

Through all of these changes, the core issues have remained the same: human equality and the right of all citizens to participate fully in a democratic society. When equality has been denied, and when the fiction of race has been used as an instrument of exclusion from the democratic polity, the result has been a society in which vast numbers of citizens—not only minorities—have had their right to fair and effective representation compromised. The lesson in that history is clear. Safeguarding our fragile democracy requires more than a battle against prejudiced attitudes and behaviors; it also demands that we uproot—at long last—a centuries-old system of power built on race and racism.

Understood in this historical context, today's arguments over voting rights are reminders that we live in a time every bit as consequential as the flush of reform that followed the Civil War. Then as now, democracy was imperiled by divisive racial appeals, violent expressions of hate, and determined efforts to undermine the right to vote. In such a moment, history has a clarifying power. It exposes the fragility of our democracy; it warns against complacency; and, in stories of struggle and courage, it offers hope that we might yet cast off the shackles of white supremacy.

Chapter 1 Race and Democracy in the Long Era of Reconstruction

We usually think of Reconstruction as the period between the end of the Civil War and the end of military occupation of the South in 1877. But that periodization is misleading, particularly in the case of North Carolina. It obscures continuities in a protracted struggle for racial equality and political democracy that spanned more than three decades, from ratification of the Thirteenth Amendment and the abolition of slavery in 1865 to black disenfranchisement and the reestablishment of white rule at the end of the nineteenth century. During this long era of Reconstruction, freedmen and a disaffected white minority forged political alliances on the basis of common economic interests and shared understandings of the rights of citizenship. In the late 1860s and again in the late 1890s, they used the ballot box to win control of both the General Assembly and the governor's office. Once in power, they reorganized state and local government according to democratic principles, liberalized election law, and expanded public investment in the welfare of fellow citizens. Together these reformers sought to build up a new order from the ruins of a society that for the better part of two centuries had been firmly anchored in the institution of racial slavery.

That project was fraught from the outset. Black North Carolinians had good reason to distrust most whites, who, if they had not owned slaves, almost certainly had aspired to do so. And for whites, who were long accustomed to equating freedom with skin color, few things posed a greater psychological threat than an association with former slaves and their descendants. Under these circumstances, it is all the more remarkable that interracial politics emerged so quickly after the Civil War and with such vibrant force. But the issues at stake made a compelling case for solidarity: equal protection of the laws and the right to

5

live without fear, a fair return on one's labor, access to education and to adequate food and housing, and an effective voice in electing representative government. All of this, of course, required free and fair access to the ballot box. The North Carolinians who fought for that right aimed to replace a white man's republic with what they called a "cooperative commonwealth," in which an injury to one was understood to be an injury to all.

War and Its Aftermath

The story of North Carolina's long reconstruction begins on the eve of the Civil War, when slaveholders ruled through a government that was more oligarchic than democratic. Eighty-five percent of lawmakers in the General Assembly were slave owners, a higher figure than in any other southern state. North Carolina's constitution granted these men their hold on power. Seats in the state senate were apportioned among fifty districts defined by the value of the taxes paid by their residents. In the state house of commons (later renamed the house of representatives), apportionment was governed by the "federal ratio," which counted slaves as three-fifths of a person. This structuring of the legislature advantaged the wealthy, slaveholding eastern section of the state. Additionally, only white men who owned one hundred or more acres of land could run for a seat in the lower chamber. Those who stood for election to the state senate were required to own at least three hundred acres, and a freehold valued at $2,000 or more was the qualifying standard for gubernatorial candidates. Oligarchic principles also shaped local government. Voters elected only two county officials: a sheriff and a clerk of court. Authority over political matters rested in the hands of justices of the peace who were nominated by the house of commons and commissioned for life terms by the governor.[1]

Taken together, these constitutional provisions removed a large majority of middling and poor whites from governance of both the state and their local communities. Even so, North Carolina's antebellum oligarchs did not rule unchallenged. In the 1850s, they faced a political revolt by white farmers in the central Piedmont and mountain west who called for removal of property requirements for the right to vote for state senators and demanded an ad valorem tax on slaveholders' human property—more than 330,000 black men, women, and children. The dissenters won the first contest by means of a popular referendum on free suffrage in 1856, and they prevailed in the second in 1861, when delegates to the state secession convention gave ground on taxation for fear that in war with the North ordinary whites "would not lift a finger to protect rich men's negroes."[2]

Those Confederate leaders must surely have had in mind the excoriating words of Hinton R. Helper, a native of Davie County. In 1857, he had put men like them on notice with a treatise titled *The Impending Crisis of the South*. Helper argued that eastern slaveholders' refusal to share political power and to invest their considerable wealth in the economic development of the central Piedmont and western backcountry served "to keep the poor whites, the constitutional majority, bowed down in the deepest depths of degradation." Though opposed to black equality, he called for the abolition of slavery—the political and economic evil that lay "at the root of all the shame, poverty, ignorance, tyranny and imbecility of the South." "Slavery must be thoroughly eradicated," Helper declared. "Let this be done, and a glorious future will await us all."[3]

The circumstances of war spread such sentiments among nonslaveholding whites. Most of North Carolina remained behind Confederate lines until the final surrender of southern forces, and for that reason the state bore a herculean share of hardship and deprivation. As resources grew scarce and conditions worsened for wives and children on the home front, North Carolina troops fled the battlefield, eventually deserting at a higher rate than soldiers from any other southern state. Many of those men received assistance from the Order of the Heroes of America, an underground network of Unionists and Quaker pacifists who were active in the Piedmont and western mountains. Food riots also broke out in North Carolina's largest towns, and in the 1864 gubernatorial election, William W. Holden, a self-made newspaper publisher, ran on a peace platform, arguing that a negotiated return to the Union offered North Carolina's only chance to "save human life" and "prevent the impoverishment and ruin of our people." Holden lost to incumbent governor Zebulon B. Vance by 58,070 to 14,491 votes, but his candidacy exposed a deep rift between the state's wealthy rulers and a significant minority of whites who had "tired of the rich man's war & poor man's fight."[4]

As the war ground on, Calvin H. Wiley, a distinguished educator and publicist, warned of the revolt that collapse of the Confederacy and the end of slavery would likely unleash. "The negroes [and] the meanest class of white people would constitute a majority," he feared, and those "who were once socially & politically degraded" would make common cause and rise up in rebellion. Signs of impending disaster were all around. In the eastern part of the state, much of which fell to Union occupation early in the war, enslaved people liberated themselves and sought refuge behind federal lines. Some took up arms against the whites who claimed to own them. In many districts, poor whites also settled scores with their "betters" by stealing livestock and crops, pillaging homes, and burning barns. One wealthy slave owner who was the target of such reprisals reported "plundering or destroying with impunity in every direction." Another was warned by landless white men that they intended to "destroy all the property and annihilate" the slaveholding class.[5]

After the Confederacy's collapse, some among North Carolina's economic and political elite despaired of the future. They most feared "being placed under our negroes—of being made the slaves of slaves." In such a condition, they would be "deprived of property of all kinds" and made into "the most downtrodden and wretched people under the sun." Others imagined that they might reclaim much of the power they wielded before the war. These men styled themselves "Conservatives" and won election to the legislature and the governor's office in late 1865. The next year, they campaigned successfully to defeat a new constitution that would have balanced political influence between the eastern and western regions of the state. Conservatives also reasserted control over black people's lives by passing legislation known informally as the Black Code. That law sought to keep blacks subjugated and to "fix their status permanently" by attaching to them the same "burthen and disabilities" imposed on free persons of color before the war. Under the Black Code, freedmen could not vote, carry weapons without a license, migrate into the state, return to the state after more than ninety days' absence, or give testimony against a white person in a court of law, except in cases in which they were either plaintiff or defendant. The law also prohibited interracial marriage; made the crime of rape or attempted rape, when committed by a black man against a white woman, punishable by death; and gave sheriffs broad authority to prosecute freedmen for vagrancy, a crime punishable by hiring out to "service and labor" (in effect, a form of reenslavement).[6]

The Republican majority in the U.S. Congress watched these developments in North Carolina and similar defiance elsewhere in the South with deepening concern. Thaddeus Stevens, congressman from Pennsylvania, warned North Carolina Conservatives that they would "have no peace until a negro is free as a white man . . . and is treated as a white man!" To that end, Congress approved the Fourteenth Amendment to the federal Constitution in June 1866 and tendered it for ratification by the states. The amendment granted birthright citizenship to freedmen and struck directly at the Black Code by guaranteeing all citizens equal protection under the law and forbidding the states to deprive any citizen of life, liberty, or property without due process.[7]

Battle over a New Constitutional Order

In North Carolina, as in all other southern states except Tennessee, Conservative lawmakers stood firm. They refused to ratify an amendment that, in their view, turned "the slave master, and the master, slave." Congress answered that defiance by asserting its authority once more, this time through passage of the Military Reconstruction Act of 1867. That legislation ordered the continued military occupation of the South, instructed army commanders to organize conventions that would rewrite the southern states' constitutions, and granted all adult male citizens— "of whatever race, or color, or previous condition of servitude"—the one-time right to vote for convention delegates.[8]

This extension of a limited franchise to black men radically altered the political landscape in North Carolina. It was now possible that an alliance between freedmen and dissenting whites could constitute a political majority. With that end in view, opponents of Conservative rule gathered in Raleigh in March 1867 to establish a biracial state Republican Party. William Holden, the Confederate peace candidate who had served briefly as provisional governor after the South's surrender, stood at the party's head and directed efforts to build a statewide organization. He used networks established during the war by the Heroes of America and by the Union League, an auxiliary of the Republican Party that recruited freedmen and sympathetic whites under the banner of "Union, Liberty, and Equality."[9]

When voters went to the polls to elect delegates to the constitutional convention, leaders of the old elite were stunned: Republicans won 107 of the convention's 120 seats. Of that majority, fifteen were black, including minister and educator James W. Hood, who had presided over the first political convention of blacks in North Carolina in late 1865. At that gathering, 117 delegates, most of them former slaves, met in Raleigh to petition white leaders for "adequate compensation for our labor . . . education for our children . . . [and abolition of] all the oppressive laws which make unjust discriminations on account of race or color."[10]

During the winter of 1867–68, delegates to the constitutional convention crafted a document that defined a thoroughly democratic polity. The proposed constitution guaranteed universal male suffrage, removed all property qualifications for election to high state office, and at the county level put local government in the hands of elected commissioners rather than appointed justices of the peace. North Carolina would no longer be "a republic erected on race and property." The constitution of 1868 also expanded the role of the state in advancing the welfare of its citizens by levying a capitation tax to fund education and "support of the poor," mandating for the first time in North Carolina history a state system of free public schools, and establishing a board of public charities to make "beneficent provision for the poor, the unfortunate and orphan." Black delegates to the convention knew that the success of these reforms would depend on safeguarding broad access to the franchise, and for that reason they backed the forceful defense of voting rights. The convention passed an ordinance to criminalize efforts to intimidate "any qualified elector of this State . . . by violence or bribery, or by threats of violence or injury to his person or property."[11]

In May 1868, voters ratified the constitution, elected William Holden governor, and gave the biracial Republican Party six of North Carolina's seven congressional seats and control of more than two-thirds of the seats in the state legislature. The scale of the Republicans' victory reflected the fact that in North Carolina the percentage of whites who crossed the color line and made common cause with former bondsmen was larger than in any other southern state.[12]

This revolutionary moment was crafted in large part by a generation of black leaders who professed a radically inclusive vision for American democracy. In 1869, twenty of those men traveled to Washington, D.C., to attend the Colored National Labor Convention, where they joined nearly two hundred other delegates from across the South and throughout the nation. Three of the North Carolinians served in elected leadership positions, including James H. Harris, who occupied the president's chair. Harris had been born into slavery in Granville County in 1832 and later left the state as a free man to study at Oberlin College. He traveled to settlements of former slaves in Liberia and Sierra Leone, helped to raise the Twenty-Eighth Regiment of U.S. Colored Troops, returned to North Carolina as a missionary teacher after the Civil War, served in both the state senate and the state house of representatives, and became an influential figure in the national Republican Party. Over the course of five days, Harris led convention delegates in drafting a manifesto for a future built on interracial cooperation, labor solidarity, and equal rights for women. The document called for unions organized "without regard to color"; extended a "welcome hand to the free immigration of labor of all nationalities"; and implored the states to fund "free school system[s] that know no distinction . . . on account of race, color, sex, creed, or previous condition." These things, the manifesto proclaimed, would make the "whole people of this land the wealthiest and happiest on the face of the globe."[13]

Back in North Carolina, white Conservatives were determined to make race, not democracy, the "central question" in state politics. They described Republicans such as Harris and his colleagues as a "mongrel mob" spawned by "negro suffrage and social disorder," and they warned nonelite whites of the loss of racial privilege. "IT IS IN THE POOR MAN'S HOUSE," the editor of the *Wilmington Journal* exclaimed, "THAT THE NEGRO WILL ENFORCE HIS EQUALITY."[14]

Such provocations struck deep chords of sentiment in a society that had been organized around racial division for more than two hundred years. But in the new order, words alone could not loosen the Republicans' hold on power. To strike the crippling blow, Conservatives turned to the Ku Klux Klan and vigilante violence. The Klan was first organized in Tennessee in 1866 and subsequently spread across the South. In North Carolina, its leader was one of the Conservatives' own: William L. Saunders, a former Confederate colonel and later a trustee of the university in Chapel Hill and secretary of state.[15]

Klan violence peaked in 1869 and 1870, as masked night riders committed "every degree of atrocity; burning houses, whipping men and women, beating with clubs, shooting, cutting, and other methods of injuring and insult." In Graham, the seat of Alamance County, they murdered Wyatt Outlaw, a black town commissioner and constable, and hung his body from a tree in the public square; and in nearby Caswell County, Klansmen lured state senator John W. Stephens, a white Republican, into the basement of the county courthouse, where they beat and stabbed him to death. Violence occurred in all parts of the state, but as the murders of Outlaw and Stephens attest, backlash against Republican interracialism was especially fierce in the central Piedmont, where the Klan aimed to intimidate not only black voters but also dissenting whites who had crossed the race line. As one Klan leader explained, he and his compatriots aimed not to restore "a white man's government only, but—mark the phrase—an *intelligent* white man's government."[16]

With the Klan marauding without constraint, Governor William Holden concluded that he had no choice but to deploy state troops to suppress the violence. In June 1870, he commissioned George W. Kirk, who had been a Union commander in Tennessee during the war, to raise a militia of nearly seven hundred men, most of them Union veterans. Then, on July 8, he declared Alamance and Caswell Counties to be in open insurrection and ordered Kirk to arrest Klan leaders. That move quelled the worst violence but gave Holden's Conservative opponents the issue they needed to win the fall election. They accused Holden of "military despotism" and compared his use of troops to Union occupation. That charge pulled some white voters back across the race line; ongoing intimidation kept others from the polls. Conservatives won majority control of the legislature in late 1870, and in early 1871 they impeached Holden and removed him from office on charges of unlawfully suspending imprisoned Klansmen's right of habeas corpus.[17]

Conservatives then set about the slow work of consolidating their hold on power and rolling back many of the reforms put in place by the state's 1868 constitution. In 1870, they proposed a constitutional convention, but voters rejected the idea. Republicans were still too formidable at the local level. But in 1874 Conservatives gained enough seats in the General Assembly to sidestep another public referendum by calling a convention with two-thirds approval in both the state house and senate. The convention met in September and early October 1875 and, with a slim Conservative majority, drafted thirty amendments. The most significant ones

- gave the General Assembly broad authority over the structure of county and municipal governments, including the power to replace elected officers with legislative appointees;
- prohibited "all marriages between a white person and a negro, or between a white person and a person of negro descent to the third generation";
- stipulated that "the children of the white race and the children of the colored race shall be taught in separate public schools, but there shall be no discrimination made in favor of, or to the

prejudice of, either race" (later enshrined by federal and state courts as the doctrine of "separate but equal");

· authorized both the use of chain gangs on "public works" and the hiring out of convict labor to third parties such as railroads and large commercial farms; and

· denied felons the right to vote.

In 1876, voters approved the amendments and elected Zebulon B. Vance to serve as governor, a post he had held for two terms during the Civil War. Across the state, Conservatives—who had now begun to call themselves Democrats—celebrated victory over what one newspaper editor earlier described as the "unwise . . . doctrine of universal equality."[18]

A year later, most federal troops—their number already drastically diminished—left North Carolina and other sections of the South. That withdrawal was partly the result of a deal in which southern Democrats in Congress won a promise to restore "home rule" in return for their agreement to settle the contested 1876 presidential election in favor of Republican Rutherford B. Hayes. Military concerns were also a factor. Federal officials redeployed troops from the South to quell labor protests in the Great Railroad Strike of 1877, which disrupted transportation from Chicago to New York and Pennsylvania, and to fight in the escalating western war against Native Americans. In the North, few whites questioned the retreat from democracy building in the South. Slavery had been abolished and secession punished. That was enough for people who had never embraced the principle of racial equality, who saw no inconsistency in hating both slavery and the enslaved. The Republican Party was also changing as it became closely aligned with the interests of big business. Its national leaders had more in common with railroad and industrial tycoons than with southern blacks and their white allies. They saw opportunity in a peaceful South, where they could partner with like-minded men and reintegrate the region into the national economy. To put it simply, profit trumped principle in what became known as America's Gilded Age.[19]

North Carolina politics soon settled into an uneasy détente. In successive elections, white Democrats polled no more than 54 percent of the gubernatorial vote, and between 1877 and 1900, forty-three black lawmakers served in the state house of representatives, eleven were elected to the state senate, and four held office in the U.S. House of Representatives. So long as black men had the right to vote, white Republicans had reason to court black allies and the two-party system re-mained competitive. Indeed, it was reasonable to believe that under the right circumstances political battle lines might again be defined more by economic interests than by racial ideology. The rise of commercial agriculture and the beginnings of industrialization provided the shock that once more produced that alignment.[20]

"For the Good of the Whole"

Economic change swept through rural North Carolina in the decades after the Civil War as large landholders and an emerging merchant class pressed freedmen and white yeoman farmers into commercial produc-tion. The result for the large majority of blacks who owned no land was the notorious system of sharecropping, which locked families into vir-tual peonage. Each spring, sharecroppers took out loans in the form of the seeds, tools, and supplies they needed in order to plant the next year's crop. To ensure repayment—often at interest rates as high as 50 percent—landlords and merchants demanded that their clients grow cotton or tobacco, which could be sold readily for cash. As farmers pro-duced more of these cash crops, prices fell and rural families spiraled downward into debt. Sharecroppers often ended the agricultural year with no profit and were unable to accumulate wealth. This process of immiseration repeated itself from generation to generation and pro-duced enduring poverty. In eastern North Carolina, where sharecrop-ping dominated the agricultural economy, the effects could be seen a century later, when blacks' per capita income in the region was as low as 22 percent that of whites.[21]

Merchants coerced many white subsistence farmers into a similar trap. On a township-by-township basis, they lobbied the state legis-lature for the passage of fence laws that took away rights to common lands on which farmers hunted, raised livestock, and harvested timber to build and heat their homes. Merchants also supported new taxes to finance the construction of railroads that linked rural communities to regional and national markets. Now, in desperate need of cash, once-independent white farmers joined their black neighbors in growing cotton and tobacco. They too fell deeply into debt, and throughout the 1880s complained loudly of merchants' campaign to rob them of "rights and liberties, which Nature's God hath given us."[22]

As conditions worsened in the countryside, farming folk began to make their way into the textile mills and tobacco factories that merchants were building in Piedmont towns and along the banks of the region's swift-flowing rivers. Most textile jobs were reserved for whites only, but with them came hardship and deprivation. In the mills, adults and young children labored for long hours and low wages. The signs of their poverty were outwardly visible. "You can tell any one who works in a cotton mill," one observer wrote. "They are always a tallow-faced, sickly set of people." In the tobacco industry, blacks had access only to the "meanest" of jobs—the work of hauling five-hundred-pound hogsheads of tobacco and cleaning and stemming the dusty, dried leaves. For that, they earned only pennies an hour.[23]

Mounting resentment over a new economic order that rewarded manipulators of credit more than cultivators of the land led farmers into revolt. Whites joined the Southern Farmers Alliance, which was first organized in Texas and then spread throughout the South by means of local chapters. Blacks affiliated with a parallel organization, the Colored Farmers Alliance. In 1892, these groups sought redress through the political process but failed at the ballot box because they acted independently of one another. Blacks remained loyal Republicans, while dissenting whites, now calling themselves Populists, gave their support to a new People's Party. The results were disastrous. In the governor's race, the Democrat won 48 percent of the vote, while the Republican and Populist candidates trailed behind with 34 and 17 percent, respectively.[24]

These numbers contained a lesson that was obvious to voters who were only a generation removed from the biracial politics of the late 1860s. Divided, the dissidents were all but certain to lose; united, they could challenge Democratic power. In 1894, Populists and Republicans in North Carolina forged a political alliance under the banner of "Fusion" and ran a joint slate of candidates. The logic of that move was clear and compelling. As one Populist explained, "We can join with others who agree with us and win a great victory." This sentiment also appealed to skilled artisans and factory laborers, black and white, who during the 1880s had rallied to the Knights of Labor and embraced the organization's call for interracial cooperation and class solidarity. On Election Day, Fusion candidates won 116 of the 170 seats in the General Assembly.[25]

A commitment to fair play and democracy animated the Fusion legislature. Lawmakers capped interest rates at 6 percent, a godsend for cash-strapped farmers who relied on credit to survive; shifted the weight of taxation from individuals to corporations; and restored elected local government, a postwar reform that Conservatives had reversed after their return to power in the 1870s. In addition, the legislature made new investments in public services that Democrats had starved for resources, including the state penitentiary, state schools for deaf and blind children, a state-supported home for black orphans, and state mental asylums.[26]

The Fusion legislature also made major revisions to state election law with the aim of guaranteeing male citizens' unobstructed access to the franchise:

- The revised law required that the clerk of the superior court in every county lay out compact precincts "so as to provide, as near as may be, at least one separate place of voting for every three hundred and fifty electors." The clerks were also instructed to publish the details of precinct boundaries and polling places in local newspapers and to post that information in public places. In a rural state in which the population was widely dispersed, these provisions ensured that neither travel nor lack of public notice would be an impediment to voting. Legislators revisited the law in 1897 to provide additional protection for the opportunity as well as the right to cast a ballot. They stipulated that every elector was "entitled," without penalty, "to absent himself from service or employment" for sufficient time to register and to vote.[27]
- To safeguard impartiality in voter registration and the supervision of elections, the law gave clerks of court—who were elected officials, and therefore accountable to voters— the authority to appoint in every precinct one registrar and one election judge from "each political party of the state." Prior to this time, that responsibility had belonged to county officers who owed their appointment and their loyalty to the majority party in the legislature.[28]
- The law also criminalized various forms of physical and economic intimidation. It specified that "no regimental, battalion or company muster shall be called or directed on election day, nor shall armed men assemble on the day of election." In addition, any person who attempted "by force and violence" to "break up or stay any election" was guilty of

a misdemeanor, punishable by imprisonment and a fine of up to $100. Similar penalties applied to "any person who shall discharge from employment, withdraw patronage from, or otherwise injure, threaten, oppress, or attempt to intimidate, any qualified voter."[29]

- The law sought to limit frivolous and obstructive challenges to voter eligibility and the legality of ballots cast by presuming the truthfulness of citizens' declarations. Challenges were allowed only on a specified day prior to an election, at which time registration books were opened for public review, and challengers were required to present proof that an elector had withheld or provided false information at the time of registration. Otherwise, the law treated "entry of the name, age, residence, and date of registration of any person by the registrar, upon the registration book of a precinct, [as] presumptive evidence of the regularity of such registration, the truth of the facts stated, and the right of such person to register and to vote at such precinct."[30]

- The law accommodated illiterate voters—23 percent of whites and 60 percent of blacks—by authorizing political parties to print ballots on colored paper and to mark them with party insignia, an old practice that Democrats had abolished. In this period, before the introduction of official, nonpartisan ballots and secret voting, electors received ballots from the party, or parties, they favored, marked through the names of any candidates they did not support, and handed their ballots to an election judge for deposit in boxes labeled with the office or group of offices for which they were voting. The use of color coding and party insignia helped illiterate voters correctly identify and cast the ballot of the party they favored. To protect voters from fraudulent handling of their ballots, the law also specified that "any ballot found in the wrong box shall be presumed to have been deposited there by mistake of the officers of election, and unless such presumption shall be rebutted, the ballot shall be counted." This was important, because there could be as many as six boxes at each polling place, and apart from their labels, they all looked alike.[31]

- Finally, the law required public disclosure of campaign financing. Every candidate had to provide, within ten days after an election, "an itemized statement, showing in detail all the moneys contributed or expended by him, directly or indirectly, by himself or through any other person in aid of his election." Those reports also were to "give the names of the various persons who received the moneys, the specific nature of each item, and the purpose for which it was expended or contributed."[32]

These changes produced momentous results in the 1896 election. Republican registration overall increased by 25 percent, and turnout among registered black voters rose from 60 to nearly 90 percent. Fusionists won more than three-fourths of the seats in the legislature and elected a white Republican, Daniel L. Russell Jr., as governor. Though Fusion insurgencies arose in other southern states, it was only in North Carolina that a biracial alliance took control of both the legislative and the executive branch of government.[33]

Fusion lawmakers used their political strength to redress two decades of Democrats' underinvestment in education. This was a particularly important issue for black Republicans, whose predecessors had led the campaign to include a mandate for public schools in the 1868 constitution and whose constituents were profoundly disadvantaged in their day-to-day interactions with landlords, merchants, and employers by an inability to read and do basic arithmetic. In 1897, lawmakers instructed county commissioners to hold elections in every school district under their supervision on the question of "levying a special district tax" for public education. Districts that voted in favor of taxation were entitled to apply for matching funds from the state. To pressure those that refused, legislators ordered an election every two years until a special tax was approved.[34]

In separate legislation, black lawmakers exercised their influence in the Fusion alliance to ensure equitable provision for students in their communities. A revised school law abolished separate white and black committees appointed at the township level to manage schools for each race and replaced them with consolidated committees made up of five appointees, no more than three of whom could come from the same political party. The law charged the new committees with managing the schools in their districts as a single enterprise. They were to appropriate funds on a strict per capita basis and to apportion "school money . . . so as to give each school in their district, white and colored, the same length of school term." Districts were also required to limit enrollments to no more than sixty-five students per school, so as to ensure a rough measure of equity in school facilities.[35]

The election and education reforms enacted in 1895 and 1897 affirmed the values that black and white reformers had written into the state constitution in 1868. That document, the core of which remains in force today, opened by invoking the Declaration of Independence and connecting the ideals of the American republic to the economic and political struggles set in motion by Confederate defeat and the abolition of slavery. Italics highlight language added by the framers of 1868: "We do declare . . . that all men are created equal; that they are endowed by their Creator with certain unalienable rights; that among these are life, liberty, *the enjoyment of the fruits of their own labor*, and the pursuit of happiness. . . . That all political power is vested in, and derived from the people; all government of right originates from the people, is founded upon their will only, and is instituted *solely for the good of the whole*." Fusion lawmakers in North Carolina, historian Morgan Kousser has observed, created "the most democratic" political system "in the late nineteenth-century South."[36]

White Supremacy and Black Disenfranchisement

Most Democrats were apoplectic. In the election campaign of 1898, they answered Fusion as they had responded to the reforms of 1868: they made white supremacy their rallying cry and employed vigilante violence as a political weapon. Responsibility for orchestrating the party's return to power fell to former congressman Furnifold M. Simmons. Simmons lived in eastern North Carolina's Second Congressional District, which was known as the "Black Second" because of its large and politically active black population. Counties in the district sent more than fifty black representatives to the General Assembly in Raleigh and elected all four of the state's nineteenth-century black congressmen, including Henry P. Cheatham, who deprived Simmons of his seat in the 1888 election. Simmons and other Democratic leaders sought to take white voters' minds off the economic and class issues that held the Fusion coalition together by raising the specter of "negro domination."[37]

Democratic newspapers took the lead in whipping up race hatred. None was more influential than the Raleigh *News and Observer*, published by Josephus Daniels. In the weeks leading up to the election, Daniels ran political cartoons on the front page of the paper to illustrate the evils unleashed by black political participation. The cartoons depicted black men as overlords and sexual predators who were intent on emasculating white men, turning them into supplicants, and ravaging their wives and daughters. Across scores of images, the *News and Observer*'s message was clear: in an inversion of the racial order, blacks had lifted themselves by pressing white men down.

Democrats wielded such racial appeals as a wrecking ball. Some Populists buckled. They gave in to the deeply entrenched ways that race shaped political and social perception and began arguing that they, not Democrats, were the most ardent defenders of white supremacy. Even so, the political battle would not be won in the press. During the closing days of the 1898 campaign, leaders of the Democratic Party turned, as they had after Emancipation, to violence and intimidation. They organized local White Government Unions and encouraged the party faithful to don the paramilitary uniform known as the "red shirt," a symbol of the blood sacrifice of the Confederacy and the late nineteenth-century equivalent of the hooded robes worn by Klansmen in an earlier era. Democrats engaged in open bullying of voters at registration and polling places across the state. In Winston, for instance, the local Republican newspaper reported that "there were crowds of men who gathered around the polls in each ward and . . . boldly drove a large per cent of the colored Republican voters and a good many white voters away from the polls."[38]

Democrats' determination to defeat their challengers at any cost was revealed most starkly in the majority-black coastal city of Wilmington. Revisions to the city charter made by the Fusion legislatures of 1895 and 1897 had undone Democratic gerrymandering and produced a Republican majority—including three blacks—on the board of aldermen. Local Democrats were enraged by that development and the fact that they would have no opportunity to unseat those officials until the next municipal election in 1899.[39]

On November 9, the day after the 1898 state election, Democratic leaders in Wilmington drew up a declaration of independence that called for the restoration of white rule in the city. They insisted "that the constitution of the United States contemplated a government to be carried on by an enlightened people; that its framers did not anticipate the enfranchisement of an ignorant population of African origin, and that those men of the State of North Carolina, who joined in forming

The Vampire That Hovers Over North Carolina.

The *News and Observer* depicted black political participation as a monster springing from the Fusion ballot box, September 27, 1898. Courtesy of the North Carolina Collection, Wilson Library, University of North Carolina at Chapel Hill.

The New Slavery.

The *News and Observer* argued that Fusion politics would produce a new form of slavery in which black men would make themselves white men's masters, October 15, 1898. Courtesy of the North Carolina Collection, Wilson Library, University of North Carolina at Chapel Hill.

A local photographer produced this souvenir postcard to document the destruction of Love and Charity Hall, the printing office of the *Daily Record*, Wilmington's black newspaper. Courtesy of the New Hanover County Public Library, Robert M. Fales Collection.

the Union, did not contemplate for their descendants a subjection to an inferior race." "The negro [has] antagonized our interest in every way, and especially by his ballot," the Wilmington *Morning Star* exclaimed. "We will no longer be ruled, and will never again be ruled, by men of African origin."[40]

The next day, armed white men under the command of former congressman Alfred M. Waddell staged the only municipal coup d'état in the nation's history. They marauded through Wilmington's black district, set ablaze the print shop of the city's only black newspaper, murdered as many as thirty black citizens in the streets, and drove the sitting board of aldermen from office in order to make room for a new, self-appointed city government with Waddell at its head.

Democrats won the 1898 election statewide by a narrow margin. They claimed only 53 percent of the vote, but that was enough to oust most Fusionists from the legislature. The victors moved immediately to "rid themselves . . . of the rule of negroes and the lower class of whites." In the 1899 legislative session, Democrats drafted an amendment to the state constitution that aimed to end biracial politics once and for all by stripping black men of the right to vote. The Fifteenth Amendment to the federal Constitution, ratified in 1870, forbade the states to restrict the right to vote on the basis of race. Now North Carolina Democrats, like their counterparts elsewhere in the South, moved to circumvent that prohibition by adopting a literacy test.[41]

In order to register to vote, male citizens would have to demonstrate to local election officials that they could "read and write any section of the Constitution in the English language." That would give Democratic registrars wide latitude to exclude black men from the polls. Democrats also included a grandfather clause in the amendment that exempted from the literacy test adult males who had been eligible to vote or were lineal descendants of men who had been eligible to vote on or before January 1, 1867. That was a magic date, because it preceded the limited right to vote given to black men under the Military Reconstruction Act, passed in March of that year. The literacy test was thus designed to achieve the very thing the Fifteenth Amendment expressly outlawed — voter exclusion based on race.[42]

Male citizens could also be denied access to the franchise if they failed to pay the poll tax levied in accordance with article 5, section 1, of the 1868 state constitution. This link between payment of the tax and the right to vote was a new impediment put in place by the disenfranchisement amendment. The amendment required that electors pay the tax before the first day of May prior to the election in which they intended to vote. That was planting time, when black sharecroppers were unlikely to have cash on hand for such a payment.[43]

Democrats rewrote state election law to boost the odds that the amendment would win approval. In the 1899 Act to Regulate Elections, they repealed reforms made by the Fusion legislatures of 1895 and 1897 and put in place new provisions that were crafted to deliver "a good Democratic majority."[44]

- With the aim of purging as many Fusion voters as possible, lawmakers ordered an "entirely new registration" in advance of the next election. In that process, registrars could, at their discretion, require an applicant to "prove his identity or age and residence by the testimony of at least two electors under oath." The law also gave "any by-stander" the right to challenge a registrant's truthfulness and force a lengthy examination.[45]
- In a reversal of provisions made in the 1895 election law, information recorded in a registration book no longer stood as presumptive evidence of an individual's right to vote. On polling

day, "any elector [could] challenge the vote of any person" on suspicion of fraud. In such cases, election officials were to question the suspect voter and compel him to swear an oath of truthfulness. But even that might not be proof enough. The law stipulated that after an oath was sworn, "the registrar and judges may, nevertheless, refuse to permit such [a] person to vote."[46]

· The 1899 law also loosened safeguards against partisanship in the management of elections. Lawmakers took the authority to appoint local election officials from the county clerks of superior court, who were directly accountable to voters, and gave it to a seven-member state elections board appointed by the Democratic majority in the legislature. That board's power was expansive. For instance, it had the authority to remove county election officials from office "for any satisfactory cause."[47]

Finally, the law put an end to practices that accommodated illiterate voters. All ballots were now to be "printed upon white paper, without ornament, symbol, or device." And if a voter or election official placed a ballot in the wrong box (there were six), it was declared void and was discarded.[48]

With the new election law in place, Democrats approached the 1900 election confident of victory. Democratic gubernatorial candidate Charles B. Aycock made disenfranchisement the centerpiece of his campaign and promised an end to what he called "nigger rule." On the stump, he offered the white electorate a new "era of good feeling" in exchange for racial loyalty. Aycock argued that black political participation had "kept the white people at enmity with each other" and that only the removal of black voters would heal the white body politic. "We must disenfranchise the negro," he explained to white voters. "Then we shall have . . . peace everywhere. . . . We shall forget the asperities of past years and . . . go forward into the twentieth century a united people."[49]

To whites who were unconvinced and blacks who were determined to resist, Aycock issued threats. "There are three ways in which we may rule," he told a white audience in eastern North Carolina. "We have ruled by force, we can rule by fraud, but we want to rule by law." To reinforce the point, bands of armed Red Shirts paraded through towns and cities in the Piedmont and the east, cheered Aycock at campaign rallies, and loitered around polling places on Election Day. The beleaguered Populist and Republican opposition could not withstand the Democratic on-

The Fraud and Force Candidate.

A Populist newspaper used Charles B. Aycock's own words to label him the "fraud and force" candidate. *Caucasian* (Clinton, N.C.), June 21, 1900.

slaught. With a turnout of 75 percent of the electors allowed to register under the revised election law of 1899, Aycock and disenfranchisement won by a 59 to 41 percent margin.[50]

Democrats cast that result as a victory of white over black, but in truth what they feared most and worked hardest to defeat was the interracial coalition that emerged from the calamity of the Civil War and reappeared in the form of Fusion. In a moment of candor, the *Charlotte*

Daily Observer admitted as much. It characterized the 1900 campaign as "the struggle of the white people of North Carolina to rid themselves of the danger of the rule of negroes and the lower class of whites." The fight in 1900 was not only to establish white supremacy but also to settle the question of which white men would rule supreme.[51]

Chapter 2 Jim Crow's Regime

The Democrats' triumph in 1900 cleared the way for a new order characterized by one-party government, racial segregation, cheap labor, and grinding poverty. With the removal of black men from politics, North Carolina's Republican Party became little more than an expression of regional differences among whites that set the western mountains, the party's surviving stronghold, against the central Piedmont and eastern coastal plain. Leaders of the Democratic Party controlled the selection of candidates through a tightly managed state convention. That arrangement, combined with the fact that no Republican had a realistic chance of winning election to a statewide office, convinced most electors that there was little reason to cast a ballot. Only 50 percent of the newly constrained pool of eligible voters turned out for the 1904 gubernatorial election. By 1912 the number had declined to less than 30 percent.[1]

Having regained control of the machinery of government, Democrats began implementing public policies that secured what one scholar has termed their "reactionary revolution." Black subjugation was at the head of their agenda. Over time, they developed an elaborate regime of law and custom that came to be known as Jim Crow, a name taken from the blackface characters in nineteenth-century minstrel shows. Most Americans—certainly most white Americans—think of Jim Crow simply as an expression of prejudice and discrimination. But it was much more than that: Jim Crow was a system of power and plunder that concentrated wealth and opportunity in the hands of the few and mobilized racial animosity in defense of that accumulation. It visited horror upon black people and immiserated vast numbers of whites as well.[2]

Black and White Apart

Lawmakers passed North Carolina's first Jim Crow law in 1899, during the same session in which they crafted the disenfranchisement amendment to the state constitution. The law required separate seating for blacks and whites on trains and steamboats. The aim of that and other such regulations—including the segregation of streetcars in 1907, legislation in 1921 that made miscegenation a felony, and a host of local ordinances that segregated drinking fountains, toilets, and cemeteries—was to mark blacks as a people apart and make it psychologically difficult for whites to imagine interracial cooperation. Segregation also divided most forms of civic space—courthouses, neighborhoods, and public squares—that might otherwise have been sites for interaction across the color line.[3]

In Charlotte, soon to be North Carolina's largest city and the hub of its new textile economy, neighborhoods in 1870 had been surprisingly undifferentiated. As historian Thomas Hanchett has noted, on any given street "business owners and hired hands, manual laborers and white-collared clerks . . . black people and white people all lived side by side." By 1910, that heterogeneity had been thoroughly "sorted" along lines of race and class. In communities large and small across the state, this process played out a thousand times over. White supremacy denied blacks access to economic and political power and erected a nearly insurmountable wall between blacks and poor whites who had risen in the mid-1890s to challenge Democrats' rule by asserting their shared grievances and claim to the franchise.[4]

Hardening racial segregation relegated the majority of black North Carolinians to the countryside and created, in effect, a bound agricultural labor force. In the 1910s, Clarence H. Poe, editor of the *Progressive Farmer*, led a movement to perfect that arrangement by proposing "territorial segregation" in rural areas and an amendment to the state constitution that would have allowed white communities to prohibit the sale of land to blacks. He modeled these proposals on policies that were being implemented in the new Union of South Africa and would lay a foundation for the system of apartheid established there in 1948.[5]

Poe believed that his reforms would lock blacks into permanent status as tenants and sharecroppers and thus make way for a "great rural civilization" to flourish among whites. He understood that the scheme might run afoul of the Fourteenth Amendment but brushed that concern aside. "If our people make up their minds that segregation is a good and necessary thing," Poe argued, "they will find a way to put it into effect—just as they did in the case of Negro disenfranchisement despite an iron-bound Amendment specifically designed to prevent it." Poe's proposal ultimately failed in the state legislature, but it had broad backing among small-scale white farmers. It also revealed how tightly

Poe and North Carolina were connected to a global movement to assert white dominion over peoples of color.[6]

Blacks who lived in cities and small towns had opportunities that were only modestly better than those available in rural areas. Most black women worked in white households as maids, cooks, and laundresses. In Durham and Winston, both tobacco manufacturing centers, and in tobacco market towns in the eastern part of the state, black women and men labored in stemmeries, where they processed the leaf before it was made into cigarettes and chewing plugs. The work was dirty and undesirable—the kind of labor that whites expected blacks to perform.[7]

Jim Crow held most black North Carolinians' earnings to near-subsistence levels. That, in turn, depressed the market value of all labor and dragged white wages downward. In textiles—North Carolina's leading industry—men, women, and children worked for some of the lowest wages in the country. Prior to the implementation of a national minimum wage in the 1930s, they earned roughly 40 percent less than workers in comparable jobs in the North. Even so, textile manufacturers often boasted that they had built their mills to save poor whites from destitution. That, they said, was also their reason for restricting most textile employment to whites only. The message to white laborers was clear: mill owners would make up for slim pay envelopes by safeguarding what W. E. B. Du Bois called the "psychological wage" of whiteness.[8]

Such insistence on maintaining the color line denied black North Carolinians something they had prized since the time of Emancipation: quality education for their children. In the 1880s, the state spent roughly equal amounts per capita on white and black students in the public schools, but by 1910 spending for blacks had fallen to 40 percent of that for whites. The state spent ten times as much on white school buildings as it did on black schools, and black teachers made only half of the $252 a year paid to whites. The results were predictable: in 1920, 24.5 percent of blacks above the age of ten were illiterate, compared to 8.2 percent of whites. Over time, racial disadvantage was persistent. Of those black children who started school in 1949, only 27.5 percent graduated from high school. The graduation rate for whites was twice that figure.[9]

Jim Crow also plagued black North Carolinians with "sickness, misery, and unnecessary death." As late as 1940, the annual mortality rate for blacks was 11.6 per thousand, compared to 7.6 per thousand for whites. Blacks were one and a half times more likely than whites to die from tuberculosis and malaria, and black infant mortality exceeded that for whites by the same margin.[10]

From all of this misery, the lords of Jim Crow's regime built great fortunes. In the early decades of the twentieth century, a ready supply of cheap labor gave them the competitive advantage to transform North Carolina from a rural agricultural state into the world's center of tobacco and cotton textile manufacturing. Half a dozen family empires dominated those industries and, together with landlords in the east, called the shots in the state Democratic Party. Journalist-historian William Snider has described this elite as an "economic oligarchy." Its members seldom ran for office themselves; instead, they depended on an allied network of corporate lawyers and bankers to manage the machinery of state. Indeed, every governor who served between 1905 and 1948 was an attorney; most graduated from the University of North Carolina and its law school; and all had close ties to manufacturing and landed interests.[11]

These men were self-styled modernizers. They promoted development of the infrastructure required to sustain North Carolina's industrial development: good roads, public education (though spending in 1920 was less than half the national average), and public health (though in 1943 the state had the nation's highest rate of health-based rejections for military service). In like manner, white leaders viewed segregation as a decidedly modern system for enforcing black North Carolinians' second-class citizenship. As Charles Aycock had pointed out in 1900, it was a means of ruling by law—though state and vigilante violence was always at the ready, should the law alone not suffice. This concern for economic growth and good order won North Carolina's political leaders praise as forward-looking moderates, at least within the southern context, but as historian William Chafe has observed, that reputation acted as "camouflage," obscuring the underlying realities of life in Jim Crow's world.[12]

The men who governed North Carolina believed in democracy and equal rights—for themselves, but not for everyone. They staunchly opposed trade unions and pitched investors on the state's abundance of cheap labor. In the late 1910s, the *Southern Textile Bulletin*, published in Charlotte, boasted of workers who were of pure "Anglo-Saxon . . . extraction—the world's master breed." They were bound to their employers by loyalty born of gratitude, and none had "any desire to become 'unionized.'" To that, the Kiwanis Club in Marion, a textile town in the western Piedmont, added, *"under no more than reasonably fair treatment of its help* [emphasis in the original], every factory or branch of industry is certain to be able to secure adequate, satisfactory and contented labor."[13]

As the *Bulletin*'s readers knew well, white supremacy was critical to the accumulation of profits, from the toil of whites as well as blacks. It was the ideology that made labor cheap and, more often than not, kept white folk content. Here too North Carolina's political leaders made their principles clear. Governor Locke Craig (1913–17) ran as an "apostle" of white supremacy, a reputation he had established as a young politician in 1898 and 1900; Governor Cameron Morrison (1921–25) campaigned proudly as a former Red Shirt who had helped to "roll back the black clouds of negroism"; Governor Clyde R. Hoey (1937–41) described efforts to pass federal antilynching legislation as a "vicious" imposition on states' rights; and Governor William W. Kitchin (1909–13) defended white supremacy as a brutal but indisputable fact of nature. "We have seen the white man come in contact with the brown man of the tropics," Kitchin observed at the dedication of a Confederate monument in 1909, "and the brown man went down. We have seen him knock at the gates of the yellow man in the East, and they opened at his will. We have seen him face the black man in his native African home, and the black man gave him the path. We have seen him press the red man, and the red man is disappearing from the face of the earth." The white man's "march has sometimes been cruel," the governor conceded, but his right to rule was undeniable.[14]

Goodbye to the Party of Lincoln

A casual observer could have been forgiven for concluding that white supremacy's victory was complete, its hold on North Carolina unassailable. Josephus Daniels—one of the regime's architects—suggested as much shortly after the 1900 election. "When Governor Aycock was elected," Daniels explained to a friend, "I said to him that I was very glad that we had settled the Negro question for all times." Aycock replied, "Joe, you are badly mistaken. . . . Every generation will have the problem on their hands, and they will have to settle it for themselves." The governor was more prescient than he might have imagined. Even at the height of Jim Crow's power, black Americans refused to surrender their claim on equal citizenship and a fair share of social resources and economic opportunity.[15]

World War I helped to put the first chinks in Jim Crow's armor. When President Woodrow Wilson spoke of a war to make the world safe for democracy, black soldiers and the communities they left behind took him at his word. More than 380,000 blacks served in the war effort, including 200,000 who went to Europe as part of the American Expeditionary Force. For many of those soldiers, putting on an army uniform was a political act. As historian Chad Williams has noted, "By fulfilling the civic obligation of military service," they "consciously staked claim to their citizenship, manhood, and place in the body politic." W. E. B. Du Bois spoke for those men as they came home from the battlefront. In May 1919, writing in the *Crisis*, the monthly journal of the NAACP, he exclaimed, "We *return*. We *return from fighting*. We *return fighting*. Make way for Democracy! We saved it in France, and by the Great Jehovah, we will save it in the United States of America."[16]

Such conviction gave some black North Carolinians the courage to step back into electoral politics. In April 1919, Raleigh physician Manassa T. Pope—himself a veteran of the Spanish-American War— joined two other black candidates, Calvin Lightner and Lawrence Cheek, in running for seats on the city council. They had the support of black civic and business leaders, whom they had mobilized in 1916 by calling a convention of black Republicans and organizing a caucus they called the Twentieth Century Voters Club. Pope and his colleagues also received the endorsement of the *Independent*, a black newspaper established in Raleigh a year later, which claimed a circulation of five thousand readers and declared on its masthead, "Standing Firm for Right— Justice for All." On Election Day, the three black candidates won just over one hundred votes apiece, out of 2,651 cast. They had expected that outcome. "We knew we wouldn't win," Lightner recalled years later, "and even if we had won, we knew the whites wouldn't let us [govern]. We just wanted to wake our people up politically."[17]

In 1920, middle-class black women organized in the same spirit. That year's election followed close behind ratification of the Nineteenth Amendment and was the first in which North Carolina women could vote. Black women had kept a low profile during debates over the amendment, but once it was ratified, they announced their intention to "share in the suffrage that will soon be granted the womanhood of our state." Many white politicians heard in that declaration a threat every bit as dangerous as Fusion. They revealed their racial and class anxiety in a fake appeal circulated by party operatives to mobilize defenders of white supremacy. The letter, published in the *Greensboro Patriot*, came from the "Colored Women's Rights Association," which, in truth, did not exist. It urged black women to register as Republicans, promising that if they did so, "all the white cotton mill operatives of the state"—who had given vent to their own grievances in a wave of wildcat strikes in 1919 and 1920—would desert the Democratic Party and join them to take control of government. As many as one thousand black women did register to vote, but a new interracial alliance—unlikely, at best—did not materialize. Indeed, Republican leaders declared their party "lily-white" and repudiated the notion that they would appeal to black voters.[18]

Prospects for opening up the political system in the Jim Crow South remained dim. But blacks who began to pour out of the region during the war found new opportunities that would transform national politics. When fighting broke out in Europe in 1914, it cut off the supply of European immigrant laborers on which the factories of the Midwest and Northeast relied. To replace them, industrial recruiters ventured south to entice sharecroppers off the land. By 1919, nearly 440,000 blacks had left in what came to be called the Great Migration. They made new homes in Baltimore, Philadelphia, New York, Pittsburgh, Chicago, and Detroit. Another 708,000 migrants followed during the 1920s. In the absence of poll taxes and literacy tests, these refugees gained access to the ballot box and influence in city politics. They also created large enclaves from which a vibrant urban black culture emerged. Literature, art, and music gave voice to the "New Negro"—a figure dignified and defiant, insistent that the nation deliver on its democratic promise.[19]

During the 1930s, the newly enfranchised migrants joined a broader black abandonment of the party of Lincoln in favor of Franklin D. Roosevelt and his New Deal. Many were at first wary of Roosevelt, a Democrat: in the South his party stood for white supremacy. But blacks were especially hard hit by the Great Depression, and the New Deal delivered much-needed relief. The largest federal jobs program, the Works Progress Administration, employed blacks in proportion to their representation in the general population and, with mixed results, attempted to prohibit discrimination in job placements and wages. Black appointees in New Deal agencies also served President Roosevelt as a shadow cabinet, and First Lady Eleanor Roosevelt publicly supported the NAACP's civil rights agenda. America remained a Jim Crow nation, but at no time since Reconstruction had the federal government held out such hope for redressing racial injustice. In his 1936 bid for reelec-

Louis Austin, editor of the *Carolina Times* (Durham, N.C.).
Courtesy of the Durham County Library Historic Photographic Archives.

tion, Roosevelt won 71 percent of the black vote in a landslide victory over Republican challenger Alf Landon.[20]

In North Carolina, newspaperman Louis E. Austin led the movement out of the Republican Party. Austin was editor of Durham's *Carolina Times*, a paper widely recognized as an exemplar of "new Negro journalism." In 1932, he helped to organize a conference of more than five hundred black business, civic, and religious leaders who met in Durham to set a new strategy for advancing black political participation. All were lifelong Republicans, deeply disgruntled with a party that had abandoned its biracial heritage. Republican president Herbert Hoover was a particular source of irritation. He won North Carolina in 1928, in part by presenting himself as a friend of white supremacy. As president, he turned a deaf ear to black suffering in the economic crisis, and in 1930, sought to broaden his appeal to southern whites by nominating North Carolina jurist and archsegregationist John J. Parker to the U.S. Supreme Court. Parker had run as a Republican candidate for governor in 1920, denouncing black voters as "a source of evil and danger."

Parker's nomination failed, but for Austin and many others at the Durham conference, it held a clear lesson: the only viable way forward was to challenge white supremacy at its root by mounting a political assault from within "the party that has the power." To that end, the conferees organized the North Carolina Independent Voters League and called for a statewide drive to add black voters to the registration rolls as Democrats, not Republicans.[21]

Josephus Daniels, editor of the *News and Observer*, railed against that effort. When several hundred blacks registered as Democrats in Raleigh, he warned that they were part of a plot "to destroy the great victory" won in 1900 under his leadership and that of Charles Aycock. "The Democratic Party in North Carolina is a white man's party," Daniels exclaimed. "It came through blood and fire in allegiance to that principle." At his urging, local election officials attempted to disqualify every black registrant—Democrat and Republican alike—but black citizens sued and won a court order to have the names of 210 restored to the voter rolls. They also taunted white Democrats. "Why," they wondered, "is it a crime for the Negro to seek to vote the triumphant ticket of the major party of the section in which he lives?"[22]

In 1936, the newly established North Carolina Committee on Negro Affairs took up the voter registration campaign. Many of its founders had attended the Durham conference in 1932, and in the spirit of that gathering they dedicated their work "to the improvement of the educational, economic, social-civic, and political welfare of Negroes" throughout the state. In the run-up to the 1936 election, the organization created "branch units" in more than a dozen towns and cities, including Wilson, Wake Forest, Greensboro, Durham, Winston-Salem, Louisburg, and Raleigh. Through coordinated efforts, these local groups increased the number of registered black voters from 22,000 to more than 60,000—most of them Democrats.[23]

The *Pittsburgh Courier* described the surge in black political participation in North Carolina as "the beginning of the 'New Deal' in the South." Registration numbers were still too low for black candidates to win election against a white opponent. But in a state that had drastically suppressed voter turnout—not only among blacks, but across the board—even a few hundred newly registered black voters who cast their ballots as a bloc could swing an election in favor of a white candidate who was sympathetic to black interests. That created an incentive for white politicians to compete for black votes and gave black voters leverage to push the Democratic Party, at the local as well as the national level, in a more progressive direction.[24]

Josiah Bailey, the senior U.S. senator from North Carolina and a veteran of the white supremacy campaigns of 1898 and 1900, defiantly opposed this incursion. In 1937, shortly after President Roosevelt's election to a second term, he threatened a congressional revolt against the New Deal. Bailey recruited southern Democrats and a number of Republicans to endorse a Conservative Manifesto that extolled the virtues of small government; called for reduced taxation of private and corporate wealth; and insisted on the primacy of "States' rights, home rule, [and] local self-government." On the Senate floor and in private exchanges, Bailey criticized President Roosevelt for "catering . . . to the Negro vote" and caricatured the New Deal as "a gift enterprise [conducted] at the expense of those who work and earn and save."[25]

In a letter to James A. Farley, chairman of the Democratic National Committee, Bailey declared that he and other southern leaders were determined "to keep negroes out of our party." Harking back to the politics of the 1860s and 1890s, he warned, "We know what their voting . . . means." Blacks would ally themselves with poor and working-class whites—people Bailey described as "common fellows of the baser sort"—and cast their ballots "for the man who promises them the most bread for the least work." Bailey gave notice that if the national Democratic Party allowed that to happen, a new "white man's party would rise in the South" to replace it. "I know very well," he said, "that I am speaking for the white race in the South, which is determined that what happened after the Civil War shall never happen again."[26]

That threat was more than empty bluster. From the outset, North Carolina Democrats had worked to blunt the New Deal's capacity to undermine Jim Crow. In Washington, they joined fellow southerners and conservative Republicans in a successful effort to exclude agricultural and domestic workers from the old-age pensions established by the Social Security Act of 1935 and the minimum wage protection afforded by the Fair Labor Standards Act of 1938. Back at home, Democratic lawmakers did all they could to limit the scope of federal jobs programs such as the Works Progress Administration. Where these programs made inroads, they tended to put upward pressure on the wages that blacks could command from private employers. For that reason, the North Carolina legislature refused to contribute the matching funds that federal officials demanded. In 1934, the Roosevelt administration called lawmakers' hand by threatening to cut relief allocations to the state. The governor reluctantly agreed to provide half of the $3 million that Washington requested, all of which he earmarked for highway construction. Even then, North Carolina continued to rank last or next to last among the states for per capita spending for work relief.[27]

University of North Carolina sociologist Guy Johnson saw in all of these actions "a tendency to perpetuate . . . existing inequalities." Blacks had made important gains, particularly in reasserting their voice in state politics, but they still lacked the power "to command a decent share of the services and benefits of government." The consequences were tragic—for blacks, most obviously, and for ordinary whites in ways that Jim Crow obscured. As Johnson argued, and as a federal report on the South later made clear, the region paid "dearly for the economic bondage and the political impotence of its black folk." Despite its vast natural resources and the productive potential of its labor force, the South's "people as a whole" were the poorest, sickest, hungriest, and least educated in the nation. For a growing group of southern liberals like Johnson, that was reason enough to replace a "policy of repression" with "fairness and justice." Doing so would make possible "better homes, better health, better living, cultural development, and human adequacy for both races." White southerners had "all to gain and nothing to lose," Johnson declared." "Self-interest, simple justice, and common-sense demand that [they] give the Negro a new deal."[28] That was not going to happen in North Carolina, at least not without a fight.

Civil Rights Unionism

When World War II erupted in Europe in 1939, it posed fresh challenges to Jim Crow's regime. Millions more blacks left the land. Some moved along familiar paths to work in the northern factories that were supplying America's allies, France and the United Kingdom; others found employment in southern cities or on the sprawling military bases that were scattered across the region. These new migrants expanded their influence within the Democratic Party, swelled the national ranks of the NAACP from 50,000 to 450,000 members, and, through the militant unions of the Congress of Industrial Organizations (CIO), gained new bargaining power on the factory floor. The federal government, concerned that racial tensions not impede the war effort, acted to limit employment discrimination and to restrain white violence.[29]

All of this played into what civil rights activists came to call a Double V strategy that encouraged black mobilization in the military and on the home front to defeat the twin evils of fascism and white supremacy. The potential for making change at home was apparent even before Pearl Harbor and the United States' formal declaration of war. In early 1941, A. Philip Randolph, president of the American Federation of Labor's Brotherhood of Sleeping Car Porters, proposed a march on Washington to pressure President Roosevelt to desegregate the military and guarantee equal employment opportunities in war industries. Noting the strength of grassroots support for the march, some observers predicted that more than one hundred thousand people would participate. Wary of any disruption in America's efforts to support its allies in their war with Germany, Roosevelt handed the organizers a partial victory. He issued Executive Order 8802, which prohibited racial discrimination in federal job-training programs and defense industry employment. With that, Randolph canceled the march.[30]

This positioning of the federal government as a potential civil rights ally gave courage to the nearly eight thousand black women and men who labored in the R. J. Reynolds tobacco factories in Winston-Salem. In 1943, they began organizing with assistance from the CIO's Food, Tobacco, Agricultural, and Allied Workers Union (FTA). Under ordinary circumstances, Reynolds would have easily crushed the effort, but the war years were anything but ordinary.

When workers staged a sit-down strike, the federal Mediation and Conciliation Service intervened to negotiate a temporary settlement. Months later, the National Labor Relations Board—a New Deal agency established in 1935 by the Wagner Act—set the ground rules for a fair election in which black workers and a significant minority of whites voted to establish a union local. Despite that result, Reynolds managers refused to sign a contract until forced by the National War Labor Board to pay higher wages and improve working conditions. Stemmery worker Ruby Jones said of that victory, "It was just like being reconstructed."[31]

Jones and others understood that winning in the workplace was but one step toward equal citizenship. Dethroning Jim Crow required that they also organize politically. "If you are going to defeat these people," union leader Robert Black explained, "not only do you do it across the negotiating table in the R. J. Reynolds Building, but you go to the city hall, you elect people down there that's going to be favorable and sympathetic and represent the best interest of the working class." To that

Officers of Local 22 of the Food, Tobacco, Agricultural, and Allied Workers Union, Winston-Salem, 1946. Original in the authors' possession.

end, the union sponsored citizenship and literacy classes and launched a citywide voter registration drive. Those efforts paid off in 1947, when black voters elected Reverend Kenneth R. Williams to the Winston-Salem Board of Aldermen. He was the first black politician in the South to defeat a white opponent at the state or local level since the Fusion era of the 1890s.[32]

The unionists in Winston-Salem and ten thousand members of a sister FTA local in eastern North Carolina's tobacco warehouses and stemmeries were in the vanguard of a statewide campaign for more inclusive politics. They provided local support for the Progressive Party, formed in 1947 by breakaway Democrats to back the presidential candidacy of Henry A. Wallace.

Wallace had served in Franklin Roosevelt's New Deal administration as vice president, secretary of agriculture, and secretary of commerce.

He established a reputation as a full-throated critic of Jim Crow and, during the early years of the Cold War, opposed hardline anticommunism as a threat to democratic values at home and abroad. In 1948, Wallace challenged Roosevelt's successor, Harry S. Truman, with demands for peaceful engagement with the Soviet Union and an immediate end to racial segregation.[33]

In North Carolina, the Progressive Party nominated a slate of candidates that represented an extraordinary commitment to equal citizenship. Of the nineteen nominees, five were white women, including journalist and civil rights activist Mary Watkins Price, the first woman to run for governor in the state. Black candidates included Reverend William T. Brown from Maxton, who opposed former governor J. Melville Broughton for a seat in the U.S. Senate; Robert E. Brown, also from Maxton, who sought election in the Eighth Congressional District, and Robert Latham, an FTA organizer in Rocky Mount, who ran in the historic "Black Second"; Durham civil rights lawyer Conrad O. Pearson, who stood for state attorney general; Gertrude Green, a tobacco worker from Kinston, and Randolph Blackwell, a student at the historically black Agricultural and Technical College of North Carolina in Greensboro (now North Carolina Agricultural and Technical State University), who sought election to the state house of representatives; and Leila B. Michael, a teacher and NAACP leader from Buncombe County, who vied for a place on her local board of education. These men and women ran on a platform that demanded repeal of North Carolina's antiunion labor laws and regressive sales tax, "civil rights for all people, improved schools, higher teacher pay, [and] increased aid to needy people." These priorities were not so different from those of Republicans of the late 1860s and the Fusion politicians of the 1890s.[34]

When Wallace stumped the state for the Progressive ticket in August 1948, bands of hecklers, sometimes numbering in the thousands and waving Confederate flags, followed his campaign entourage from town to town and pelted them with eggs and tomatoes. Shouts of "nigger lover" filled the air and were echoed in more genteel terms by the state's newspapers. The editors of the *Charlotte Observer* suggested that Wallace and his compatriots had brought the trouble on themselves by announcing in advance that the candidate "would speak to none but unsegregated audiences."[35]

Wallace gave his detractors no quarter. In a 1947 speech, he had declared that "Jim Crow in America has simply got to go." His reasoning echoed a long tradition of dissent within North Carolina and the South: "The dangerous disease of race hate, which bears so heavily upon Negro citizens . . . at the same time drags the masses of southern white citizens into the common quagmire of poverty and ignorance and political servitude. . . . Jim Crow divides white and Negro for the profit of the few. It is a very profitable system indeed."[36]

The price exacted by Jim Crow was measured not just in dollars, but in lives as well. Wallace made that point with a "single, grim fact": "A Negro child born this day has a life expectancy ten years less than that of a white child born a few miles away." "These ten years," he explained, "are what we are fighting for. I say that those who stand in the way of the health, education, housing, and social security programs which would erase that gap commit murder. I say that those who perpetuate Jim Crow are criminals. I pledge you that I shall fight them with everything I have." Wallace understood the fury his words would provoke. "Every uttered truth," he observed, "produces a tremor in those who live by lies."[37]

The Progressive Party's defeat in 1948 was a foregone conclusion. Wallace's position on race and anticommunism alienated too many white voters. But the electorate was restless. They gave the keys to the governor's mansion to W. Kerr Scott, a new kind of Democrat. He was a farmer from Alamance County, located in the central Piedmont, who had served as commissioner of agriculture for twelve years and ran in the Democratic gubernatorial primary without the endorsement of the party's power brokers—the manufacturers, lawyers, and bankers who, since 1900, had anointed their favored candidates. As journalist Rob Christensen has observed, Scott reassembled "the old coalition of the Populists in the 1890s—small white farmers and blacks." He appealed to rural voters of both races by promising much-needed infrastructure improvements: better farm-to-market roads and the extension of electric power and telephone lines to households that had neither. Scott also courted white textile workers by criticizing the industrialists who acted as "kingmakers" in the Democratic Party. "It amounts to oligarchy when a ring-controlled candidate can be pushed into the highest office in the state against the people's wishes."[38]

Perhaps most important, Scott was masterful at fudging the race issue with white voters. Among friends, he often told a story of campaigning in the eastern part of the state. At a country store, he met a local political boss who asked, "How do you feel about this here race situation?" Scott recalled, "I was in a pickle. . . . I needed votes from the

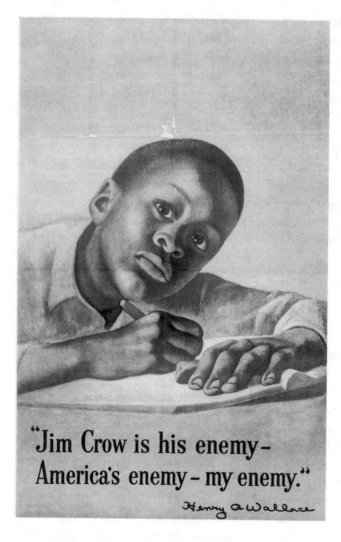

Henry A. Wallace campaign poster, 1948. Courtesy of M. H. Ross Papers, Georgia State University Library Digital Collections, http://bit.ly /2xmw2R6.

colored folks and I needed them from the whites." So he said, "Let me put it this way mister. I'm a North Carolina Democrat. I was born south of the Mason-Dixon line. . . . My daddy before me was a southerner, and a North Carolina Democrat. Does that answer your question?" Scott's evasiveness was convincing. "By golly, that's good enough for me," the man replied.[39]

Scott's election marked the emergence of a progressive faction within North Carolina's Democratic Party. His Go Forward program included new state investments in schools and rural highways that marked "the largest expansion in government services in a generation." Scott called, unsuccessfully, for repeal of the state's antiunion right-to-work law and passage of its first minimum wage legislation. In his first year in office, he also appointed Harold L. Trigg, president of St. Augustine's College, to serve as the first black member of the State Board of Education. Though Scott did not question segregation, he declared at a gathering of dairy farmers, "It is time North Carolina stopped dodging the Negro question. I'm going to follow through and see that the minority race has a fair opportunity and gets the training to fit into the industrial and agricultural life of the State." Blacks deserved fair treatment, he said. "They came here against their will, brought in chains."[40]

That was all well and good, but conservatives in the Democratic Party did not surrender. In the 1950 U.S. Senate campaign, they once again unleashed the full fury of the politics of white supremacy.

"An Insult to the Intelligence of the Good People of North Carolina"

The story of the 1950 election began a year before, when Senator J. Melville Broughton died in office. Governor Scott appointed University of North Carolina president Frank Porter Graham to fill the post until the next election. Graham's liberal views were well known. He was an outspoken supporter of labor unions and proposed a workers' "bill of rights" during textile strikes that rocked the state in the late 1920s; President Roosevelt appointed him to the White House advisory council that shaped the Social Security Act of 1935; he chaired Roosevelt's Advisory Committee on Economic Conditions in the South, which documented widespread poverty in the region; and in 1938, he served as founding president of the Southern Conference for Human Welfare, an interracial organization devoted to "equal and exact justice to all" (a phrase borrowed from President Thomas Jefferson's 1801 inaugural address).[41]

In the 1950 Democratic primary, Graham's chief rival was Willis Smith, a respected corporate lawyer from Raleigh. Smith had close ties to the North Carolina Citizens Association, organized in 1942 by a group of conservative business leaders. The association's forty-seven founding directors represented every sector of the state's economy. The roster included Richard G. Stockton, vice president of Winston-Salem's Wachovia Bank and Trust Company; eastern North Carolina industrialist Edwin Pate, who had a stake in multiple enterprises that included agricultural supply companies and small-town department stores; and Lloyd E. Griffin, an attorney and former state legislator who acted as a go-between for Democratic Party power brokers and owners of the state's largest textile and tobacco manufacturing firms. J. Melville Broughton, who at the time occupied the governor's office, addressed the association's first meeting. He assured the group that under his administration the state would no longer "play Santa Claus for the sort of people" who had grown accustomed to the supposed largesse of New Deal jobs programs.[42]

Observers of state politics compared the Citizens Association to the American Liberty League, which national business elites had organized a decade earlier to oppose the New Deal. Its founders included members of the du Pont family; Alfred P. Sloan, president of General Motors; Pittsburgh industrialist and financier Andrew W. Mellon; and J. Howard Pew, president of Sun Oil. The league attempted to wrap itself in a cloak of populist outrage, but its work was shaped at every turn by the interests of corporate America. With a budget and headquarters staff larger than those of the Republican Party, the league mounted a campaign—on the stump, in print, and over the radio—that disparaged New Deal jobs programs for the unemployed and federal protection for labor unions as instruments of social leveling based on communist principles.[43]

During the 1940s and 1950s, the North Carolina Citizens Association made a similar, though quieter, case for small government, low taxes, union-free workplaces, and limited investment in public education and other forms of social provision. Like the Liberty League, the association presented itself as defender of the people's interests, but it supported public policies that left North Carolinians poor and poorly educated. In the early 1950s, only 9.5 percent of citizens over the age of twenty-five had completed four years of high school, compared to a national average of 20.2 percent, and North Carolina workers earned the lowest manufacturing wages in the country—$48.88 a week, on average, compared to $71.86 for workers nationwide. The Citizens Association's complicity in those circumstances so irked Governor Kerr Scott that he suggested changing the name of the group's magazine from *We the People* to *We the People against the People*.[44]

As a representative of North Carolina's conservative business interests, Willis Smith sought to discredit the reform-minded politics that had put Scott in office and had made Frank Graham a much-admired public figure. He cast Graham as a communist sympathizer and radical proponent of racial equality. When Smith opened his campaign in eastern North Carolina, he riffed on Senator Joseph McCarthy's hunt for communist agents and Graham's affiliation with a host of left-leaning causes. "I do not now nor have I ever belonged to any subversive organizations," Smith declared, and "as a United States Senator I shall never allow myself to be duped into the use of my name for propaganda or other purposes by those types of organizations." The Smith campaign sharpened the attack with newspaper ads that associated Graham with Earl Browder, former chairman of the Communist Party USA, and postcards mailed from New York that carried a fake endorsement of Graham by NAACP executive secretary Walter White. These insinuations ate away at Graham's advantage as the incumbent candidate. On Election Day, he won 48.9 percent of the vote and Smith finished second with 40.5 percent.[45]

Since Graham failed to achieve a majority, Smith was entitled to call for a runoff. At first, he hesitated; he was unsure that he could raise the money to finance another campaign or that he had the stamina for such a contest. Then, on June 5, just days before the deadline for Smith's decision, the U.S. Supreme Court handed down rulings that affirmed black students' right to equal access to publicly funded graduate education and banned segregation on railroads. The court's actions galvanized Smith's supporters. On the afternoon of June 6, Jesse Helms, a young news director for WRAL Radio in Raleigh, made arrangements to air at fifteen-minute intervals a plea for Smith backers to rally at his home and urge him to stay in the fight. Smith had heard similar encouragement from friends and colleagues in the North Carolina Citizens Association. The next morning, he called for a second primary.[46]

The political battle that followed was the rawest since 1900. The Smith campaign focused particularly on Graham's service in 1946–47 on President Harry Truman's Committee on Civil Rights, which issued the first federal report on racial inequality and laid the groundwork for Truman's desegregation of the military a year later. The report, titled *To Secure These Rights*—a deliberate reference to the Declaration of Independence—called unequivocally for "the elimination of segregation, based on race, color, creed, or national origin, from American life."[47]

To that end, the report urged the president to establish a permanent Fair Employment Practices Committee (FEPC) to monitor and root out racial discrimination in the workplace. Frank Graham—who preferred moral suasion over government intervention as an instrument of social change—had dissented from that part of the report, but the Smith camp paid no mind. They warned that such an agency would impose

Did **YOU** know **?**

Over **28**% of the population of North Carolina is COLORED

FEPC, if enacted, means more than that you might be working next to and sharing facilities with some one not of your choice . . . and probably not of your employer's choice, either.

It means that if you are working in a plant that employs 1,000 people, 280 of them will be someone besides you or your friends.

If you work in a plant employing 375 people, 105 of them won't be you or your friends.

Or, if you just work where there are three people, one of them won't be you or your present associates.

This is not a pretty picture . . . but these are the facts.

Do not be fooled . . . most of all, do not be lulled by sweet words of high-flown idealists.

The SOUTHERN WORKING MAN *MUST NOT BE SACRIFICED* to vote-getting ambitions of political bosses!

A Vote for *Willis Smith* | SATURDAY JUNE 24th | . is a Vote for *Your* Freedom

WORKING MEN FOR SMITH COMMITTEE

A flier produced by Willis Smith's campaign warned that a permanent Fair Employment Practices Committee would set racial quotas and take jobs away from white workers. Courtesy of the Daniel Augustus Powell Papers, Southern Historical Collection, Wilson Library, University of North Carolina at Chapel Hill.

racial quotas in all areas of employment and take away the livelihood of nearly a third of white workers. "Did you know," one Smith handbill asked, that "over 28% of the population of North Carolina is colored?" The implied assumption was that under imagined FEPC rules an equal percentage of jobs would be set aside for blacks. "[This] means that if you are working in a plant that employees 1,000 people," the handbill continued, "280 of them will be *someone besides you or your friends.*" Another broadside cautioned that once race mixing began in the workplace, it would quickly spread to buses, cabs, and trains; hotels and rooming houses; restaurants, schools, and toilets. "White People Wake Up Before It's Too Late!" the broadside exclaimed. "Frank Graham Favors Mingling of the Races."[48]

Graham's supporters answered by pointing to the class interests that drove Smith's defense of Jim Crow. They warned white working people that Smith would roll back the hard-won economic gains of the New Deal, and they framed the issues in the campaign as rich versus poor rather than black over white. A newspaper advertisement reminded readers that Graham had a forty-year record of "leadership for better

Frank Graham's backers argued that Willis Smith stirred up "race hatred" to convince whites to vote "against their own best interests." *News and Observer* (Raleigh, N.C.), June 22, 1950.

(Political Advertisement)

Why, Mr. Smith?

Why do <u>YOU</u> *attempt to fan the flames of RACE HATRED?*

Why do <u>YOU</u> *shout and holler so much against the Negro?*

Why, Mr. Smith?

Is It Because

you wish to CONCEAL the fact that you were AWOL in the fight for better schools and roads?

Is It Because

you wish to CONCEAL your publicly stated belief that 40 cents an hour is too much pay for N. C. workers?

Is It Because

you wish to CONCEAL the fact that in every fight for the betterment of all our people you preferred to spend your time in the interests of the 36 CORPORATIONS which employ you?

Is It Because

you wish to CONCEAL the fact that you are supported by Republicans who put our farmers in Hoover carts and our wage earners in breadlines?

Is It Because

you have so little faith in the people of North Carolina that you think they can be duped by Talmadge tactics to vote against their own best interests?

Is It Because

you wish to CONCEAL, Mr. Smith, that you are a REACTIONARY who is AFRAID — AFRAID of the future, AFRAID of the progressive program of the Democratic Party, AFRAID of our American Democratic destiny?

VOTE for the FUTURE
IN
FRANK P. GRAHAM

Wake County Committee for Graham
Wm. Joslin, Chairman

schools, roads, and hospitals," all of which benefited "the weak, the underprivileged, and little people of N[orth] C[arolina]." These efforts were largely unsuccessful, in part because Graham refused to challenge his opponent's integrity by calling out misrepresentations of his past.[49]

On Election Day, a majority of voters rallied to the maintenance of white rule and rejected Frank Graham's vision for a just and equitable South. Smith won the second primary by more than nineteen thousand votes. He traveled to Washington to take his Senate seat in 1951 and carried Jesse Helms with him as a member of his staff. Twenty-two years later, Helms would return as a Republican senator and leader of a conservative movement that came to be known as the New Right.[50]

Kerr Scott denounced "the injection of the race issue" into the 1950 contest as "an insult to the intelligence of the good people of North Carolina." Jonathan Daniels, who had taken the helm of the *News and Observer* from his father, Josephus, recognized something more menacing. It was the use of "cold-blooded, advertising agency technique to arouse prejudices for the purpose of reactionary politics." Jonathan obviously ignored his father's sophisticated use of graphic racial appeals in the white supremacy campaigns of 1898 and 1900. Even so, it is hard to imagine a more portentous description of our politics today.[51]

Chapter 3 The Forgotten Fifties

In the aftermath of the 1950 election, Frank Graham's supporters were distraught. "I weep for the people of North Carolina," one woman wrote, "because they [were] swayed by prejudices [and] lies." But editor Louis Austin found cause for hope, even as he mourned Graham's defeat. He reminded his readers that more than 260,000 voters—the vast majority of them white—had cast their ballots for Graham, and in doing so had refused to bow to "race hatred." Despite obvious similarities, Graham's loss was not a calamity on the same scale as the defeat of Fusion half a century before. Black mobilization and appeals to justice and decency had loosened Jim Crow's grasp and created new room for civil rights activists to maneuver. Austin urged his readers to seize the moment by lighting a "torch of freedom" that would "send bright rays into the dark corners of [a] benighted State."[1]

Leaders and ordinary folk in black communities across North Carolina took up that challenge. In 1951, a "rush" of thirteen black candidates stood for election in eleven cities, from Rocky Mount in the east to Winston-Salem in the Piedmont. Three of them won seats on their municipal councils.[2] Two years later, twenty-four black candidates ran in nineteen cities, and six bested their white opponents.[3]

The victories in 1953 were, in many respects, predictable. With one exception, they occurred in Piedmont cities with substantial black populations and active black civic organizations. In Winston-Salem, unionized tobacco workers had spurred voter registration and created a political movement that continued to elect a black candidate to the city's board of aldermen. Black business leaders in Durham had similar success. Under the auspices of the city's Committee on Negro Affairs, they had been registering voters and sponsoring candidates for the better part of two decades. In 1953, they broke through with the election of Rencher N. Harris, a real estate appraiser, to the city council. Harris also had the backing of a short-lived interracial alliance of progressive whites and unionized textile and tobacco workers.[4]

More surprising, and ultimately more threatening to white rule, was the fact that seven black candidates had the courage to seek office in eastern North Carolina, where Jim Crow was most deeply entrenched, and that in Wilson, a small tobacco market town located in that section of the state, George K. Butterfield Sr. won election to the board of commissioners. Through the end of the decade, this spread of civil rights activism beyond the cities of the Piedmont tested white politicians' ability to deflect black claims on equal citizenship.

The story of George Butterfield's political career epitomized the contest between white men in power and their black challengers. Butterfield was a dentist and a veteran of World War I, born in Bermuda and educated at Meharry Dental College in Nashville, Tennessee. He moved to Wilson in 1928 and quickly established himself as a leader in the city's black community. George K. Butterfield Jr., who currently represents North Carolina's First Congressional District, remembers that his father "was always a thorn in the side of the white . . . establishment." In the 1940s, the elder Butterfield and his brother-in-law, Fred Davis Jr., directed a number of voter registration drives. They recruited brave volunteers and sat "up the night" with them to memorize and "rehearse the Constitution." When those aspiring voters took the literacy test, "some would pass and some would not," because the outcome was "just the whim of the registrar." Progress was slow, but over time, the effort paid off. By 1953, more than five hundred of Wilson's black citizens had qualified to vote.[5]

That figure was large enough to convince Butterfield to stand for election as a town commissioner representing Wilson's Third Ward. Although blacks constituted a majority in the ward, whites outnumbered them among registered voters. Butterfield's supporters overcame that disadvantage by turning out at a much higher rate than their white neighbors. When ballots were counted, Butterfield and his opponent each received 382 votes. As stipulated in Wilson's town charter, election officials decided the winner by drawing lots. A blindfolded child pulled Butterfield's name from a hat.[6]

Butterfield used his political office to press for improved municipal services in Wilson's black neighborhoods, additional funds for black schools, and the desegregation of recreational facilities, including the town's minor-league baseball stadium. After he won reelection in 1955, Wilson's white commissioners moved to be rid of him. Shortly before the 1957 election, they approved a surprise resolution to change from a ward system to an at-large form of municipal government in which a

George K. Butterfield Sr. (second from left) taking the oath of office as a Wilson town commissioner. Courtesy of Congressman G. K. Butterfield, http://bit.ly/2Q3hKLA.

full slate of commissioners would be elected in a single, multicandidate contest. Under that arrangement, a black candidate would face not one but many white opponents.[7]

The state legislature quickly approved the change and added a provision to Wilson's charter that prohibited single-shot voting, or, as it was sometimes called, bullet voting. That was the practice of marking a ballot for only one candidate in multicandidate contests in which the top vote getters won election to a set number of open seats. In simple mathematical terms, single-shot voting offered black voters—always a minority—their best chance at electing representatives from their communities. The new prohibition undercut that prospect by requiring that election officials discard single-shot ballots.[8]

These changes in Wilson's town government denied Butterfield a third term. In the 1957 election, he placed eighth in a field of sixteen candidates who vied for six seats on the town commission. Four years later, Reverend Talmadge A. Watkins, Butterfield's pastor and political ally, ran for a commission seat and, after losing, challenged the anti-single-shot rule in a lawsuit. North Carolina's Supreme Court ultimately decided the case, *Watkins v. City of Wilson*, in favor of the defendants.

The justices wrote: "It is an established principle that to entitle a private individual to invoke the judicial power to determine the validity of executive or legislative action he must show that he has sustained, or is immediately in danger of sustaining, a direct injury as the result of that action and it is not sufficient that he has merely a general interest common to all members of the public." Watkins did not meet that standard, because "even if credited with all rejected ballots, he would not have enough votes to change the [election] result." In 1962, the U.S. Supreme Court declined to review the case on appeal.[9]

Watkin's defeat in court validated the work of white politicians who had been busy restructuring local government across eastern North Carolina. Between 1955 and 1961, the state legislature approved a flurry of new laws that mandated at-large voting in a shifting mix of elections for county boards of commissioners and town councils in twenty-three eastern counties. In each of those places, lawmakers also prohibited single-shot voting. As a reporter for the *News and Observer* later noted, the purpose of these measures was "to slow the growth of black political power."[10]

With no sense of irony, white politicians defended these measures as protection against the corrupting influence of "bloc" interests, particularly those defined by race. That was a well-worn rationale. For instance, a group of Willis Smith's supporters had charged in 1950 that "bloc voting by any group is a menace to democracy." In an advertisement published in the *News and Observer*, they turned to Charles Aycock—one of the original architects of white supremacy—as their authority on the matter. In his 1901 inaugural address, Aycock had justified his party's use of political violence by pointing to heavily black counties in the east, where, he claimed, "120,000 negro votes cast as the vote of one man" had threatened the "security of life, liberty, and prosperity."[11]

The hypocrisy of such historical claims infuriated *Carolina Times* editor Louis Austin. He noted that since the end of slavery, blacks had found the "biggest 'bloc' of . . . all . . . arrayed against them." It included "leaders of the Ku Klux Klan," politicians who "continuously fanned the flames of race hatred," and the "mass of white voters" who elected them. Together, these enemies of democracy barred blacks from political office and denied them both "equal education [and] equal employment opportunities." Such actions left blacks no alternative but to vote their group interests, or as Austin put it, to "look principally to [their] own tents for whatever advancements" might be made.[12]

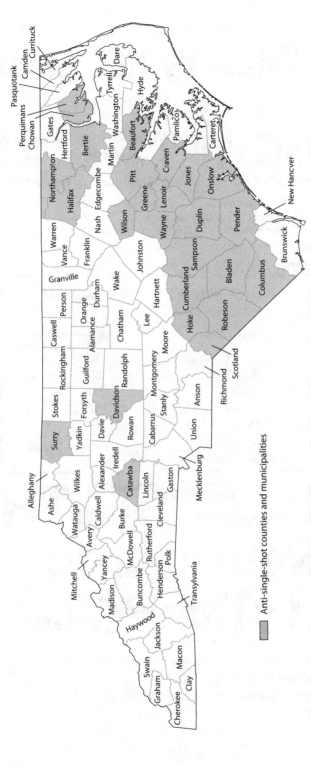

Between 1955 and 1961, the General Assembly outlawed single-shot voting in a mix of countywide and municipal elections in twenty-three eastern counties, all of which had large black populations. The prohibition also applied to three counties in the western Piedmont that were Republican strongholds.

Anti-single-shot counties and municipalities

Bloc Voting By ANY Group

Is A

MENACE TO DEMOCRACY

Governor Charles B. Aycock said this in his Inaugural Address, January, 1901:

"When we came to power (1898), we desired merely the security of life, liberty and prosperity. We had seen all these menaced by 120,000 Negro votes cast as the vote of one man."

Here is what happened on May 27th, 1950—

BLOC VOTING BY NEGROES IN NORTH CAROLINA:

(OFFICIAL RETURNS)

	Precinct.	GRAHAM.	SMITH.
RALEIGH	No. 10	493	9
	No. 16	518	18
DURHAM	Hillside	1514	7
	Pearson School	1187	8
GREENSBORO	No. 5	1231	12
CHARLOTTE	No. 2	512	11

THESE ARE RETURNS FROM ONLY SIX NEGRO PRECINCTS

WILLIS SMITH

Represents

ALL The People

Sampson Committee for Willis Smith
Marvin Wooten, Chairman

A Willis Smith campaign ad invoked Governor Charles B. Aycock to warn against the threat of black "bloc" voting. *News and Observer* (Raleigh, N.C.), June 22, 1950.

Challenging Jim Crow in Court

The guardians of white rule were shrewd adversaries who displayed their resourcefulness not only at polling places but also in courts of law. That was perhaps nowhere more apparent than in the adjudication of a series of lawsuits brought by James R. Walker Jr., a young black attorney from eastern North Carolina. Walker grew up in Hertford County, located in the historic Second Congressional District, where black political strength had been concentrated in the decades after Emancipation. His parents, James and Ethel, were teachers who instilled in their son a determination to "fight social injustice." After serving in the U.S. Army during World War II, the younger Walker set out to become a civil rights lawyer.[13]

In 1949, Walker applied for admission to the school of law at the University of North Carolina in Chapel Hill but was rejected on account of his race. With no other option, he enrolled at the North Carolina College for Negroes (now North Carolina Central University), where state lawmakers had established a separate and decidedly unequal law school to protect the white university from desegregation. But within a year, the U.S. Supreme Court changed the game. The court ruled in a Texas case, *Sweatt v. Painter*, that racially segregated programs of graduate and professional education were acceptable only if they exhibited "substantive equality." On the basis of that judgment, four black plaintiffs— Harvey Beech, James Lassiter, J. Kenneth Lee, and Floyd McKissick— sued in federal court and won admission to the law school in Chapel Hill. They, along with Walker, who had applied at the same time, began their studies during the summer of 1951. Walker, Lee, and Beech took their degrees a year later and became the University of North Carolina's first black graduates.[14]

In 1955, black community leaders in Halifax County persuaded Walker to return to eastern North Carolina and join their struggle for political rights. When he opened his law office in Weldon, he was the only black attorney in a six-county area where sharecropping still bound black families to the land and racial violence was a fearsome fact of life. Walker was unafraid. "I was an Army man," he remembered. "Had been to the front. . . . I wasn't scared of nothing."[15]

Walker drew financial and professional support from a small community of black lawyers in North Carolina's Piedmont cities. He also built a loose network of black preachers, teachers, businessmen, and

James R. Walker Jr. as a third-year law student at the University of North Carolina, *Yackety Yack*, 1952. Courtesy of the North Carolina Collection, Wilson Library, University of North Carolina at Chapel Hill.

club women from twenty-five eastern counties. He called the group the Eastern Council on Community Affairs. Its members gathered news of voter infringement, mobilized to confront hostile white election officials, and helped Walker identify plaintiffs who were prepared to challenge Jim Crow in court.[16]

Walker began filing lawsuits in 1956. In one of his first cases, he sued on his own behalf to challenge the prohibition of single-shot voting in an at-large election for seats on the Halifax County Board of Education. Officials had discarded his ballot because he cast a single vote for the one black candidate rather than comply with instructions to choose seven of eight contenders.

The case eventually made its way to the North Carolina Supreme Court, where Walker ran afoul of state lawmakers' efforts to stall school desegregation. In 1955, quick on the heels of the U.S. Supreme Court's *Brown* decision, they extended their influence over policy at the local level by making seats on county school boards appointed rather than elected positions. Under the new arrangement, political parties continued to hold primary elections, but the results were no longer binding. County boards of elections reported the winners to the state superintendent of public instruction, who in turn sent their names to the legislature in the form of nominations. Lawmakers then appointed school board members as they saw fit. By time the high court heard Walker's appeal, lawmakers had already exercised their authority to appoint members of the Halifax school board. In light of that fact, the court ruled that "questions raised by plaintiff are now moot" and dismissed Walker's case.[17]

While litigating his personal complaint in Halifax County, Walker filed another lawsuit on behalf of Louise Lassiter, a resident of nearby Northampton County who had been denied the right to register after failing to prove that she was literate. At the time, registrars enjoyed broad authority to administer literacy tests in whatever form they imagined. They often framed the tests as civics exams that reached well beyond a simple assessment of an applicant's ability to read and write. Observers throughout eastern North Carolina documented a "bewildering variety" of questions. Can you "name the signers of the Declaration of Independence?" a registrar might ask. "What is *habeas corpus*?" "If the NAACP attacked the U.S. government, on which side would you fight?" "Explain how a person [can] be imprisoned for debt in North Carolina, who created the world, and what 'create' mean[s]." Louise Lassiter failed her test because she mispronounced words from the state constitution, including the term "indictment."[18]

Lassiter's case set off alarm bells in Raleigh, where state officials worried that she might prevail in federal court. Her complaint coincided with passage of the Civil Rights Act of 1957, the first national legislation of its kind since 1875. The law established the U.S. Civil Rights Commission to investigate allegations of voter suppression and authorized the Department of Justice to institute civil action against any person who interfered with the right of another "to vote or to vote as he may choose."[19]

Just days before Lassiter's case was scheduled to be heard in U.S. district court, legislators revised state election law to make the literacy test less arbitrary. They struck the requirement that literacy be proven "to the satisfaction" of registrars and created an appeals process for citizens who failed the test—though complaints would be heard only if filed "by 5:00 p.m. on the day following the day of denial." These changes were enough to satisfy the federal court, which declined to proceed with Lassiter's case until she had petitioned for a local remedy.[20]

Soon after the court's decision, Lassiter made another attempt to register. But this time, at Walker's instruction, she refused examination on grounds that the literacy test violated her right to vote. That focused Lassiter's legal complaint on the constitutionality of the test itself rather than the method of its administration. When the case reached the North Carolina Supreme Court, lawyers for the Northampton County elections board argued in circles. They denied that the literacy test was discriminatory on account of race and then defended it as a political necessity adopted to correct the "outrages perpetrated upon the people of this State during the Tragic Era of Reconstruction," when the ballot was "placed in the hands of illiterate people . . . supported by the armed might of the Federal Government." Convinced by such reasoning, the court rejected Lassiter's constitutional claims. It found no evidence of "discrimination in favor of, or against any [person] by reason of race, creed, or color."[21]

On appeal in 1959, the U.S. Supreme Court unanimously affirmed that ruling. Writing for the court, Justice William O. Douglas acknowledged that when arbitrary authority was vested in registrars, a literacy requirement could "make racial discrimination easy." But he found no evidence of that intent in North Carolina's election law as amended in 1957. He instead read literacy tests as an expression of the state's desire "to raise the standards for people of all races who cast the ballot." Ignoring the effects of a century of school discrimination in the South and the core reasoning of the 1954 *Brown* decision, Douglas insisted that "literacy and illiteracy are neutral on race, creed, color, and sex, as reports around the world show."[22]

Blacks certainly had no natural inclination to illiteracy, but the connection between illiteracy and race as a social category and lived experience was undeniable. Had Justice Douglas examined conditions in Northampton County, that harsh reality would have been readily apparent. Grinding poverty and a long history of discriminatory spending on schools meant that large numbers of blacks were denied even a rudimentary education. In 1950, black adults in Northampton County had completed, on average, 5 years of schooling. That compared to 5.9 years for black adults and 8.6 years for white adults statewide. These figures meant that a considerable portion of voting-age blacks, in Northampton County and across the state, had completed fewer than the three years of education that demographers assumed was required to develop basic literacy skills.[23]

In 1960, Walker returned to court with a new client. Having failed to win a judgment that the literacy test was unconstitutional per se, he revisited the question of how it was administered. His client, Bertie County resident Nancy Bazemore, had been denied by a registrar who required that she write down passages from the state constitution as he read them aloud. Bazemore failed because of spelling errors. When the case reached the state supreme court, the justices ruled in Bazemore's favor and issued guidelines that sharply limited registrars' discretion in determining the form and content of the literacy test. They instructed those officials to evaluate "nothing more" than applicants' ability to "utter aloud" a section of the state constitution and to write it out "in a reasonably legible hand." Furthermore, the test was to be based on a printed copy of the constitution rather than a registrar's dictation, and there were to be no penalties for "the occasional misspelling and mispronouncing of more difficult words."[24]

The *Bazemore* decision represented what many observers came to view as the North Carolina way in managing black demands for equal rights. It rejected naked discrimination and insisted on "fair" and "impartial" enforcement of the law, but also left room for sorting citizens into racial categories. Across North Carolina, most whites registered and voted without a literacy test. They "took it for granted" that they were entitled to do so because of the color of their skin. In Nancy Bazemore's home county, one registrar was forthright. When asked if any whites had failed the literacy test, he replied, "No. I mean I didn't have any to try it." Though the state supreme court did not address this issue directly, it validated the underlying assumption by ruling that there was no legal requirement that every registrant be examined. "It would be unrealistic to say that the test *must* be administered to all applicants," the justices wrote. "The statute only requires that the applicant *have* the ability [emphasis in the original]" to read and write. "If the registrar in good faith knows that [the] applicant has the requisite ability, no test is necessary."[25]

This reading of state election law meant that registrars still possessed the authority to group citizens into two classes: whites, who were assumed to be literate, and blacks, who had to prove it. The law did not require that the literacy test be administered to all citizens on an equal basis, only that it "be administered, where uncertainty of ability exists, to all alike." That was a notably pernicious doctrine in a white man's society long habituated to the idea that blacks, by their very nature, lacked the intellectual and moral capacity to function as citizens.[26]

North Carolina's response to black demands for political rights was adaptive, not reactionary. It stood apart from what became known as "massive resistance" elsewhere in the South. As one contemporary observed, it was a "subtle strategy" for preventing "the black vote from being effective." White political leaders were willing to tolerate the registration of a limited number of black voters and even the occasional election of a black officeholder, but they conceded nothing on the foundational principles of Jim Crow: black inferiority and second-class citizenship. This was their way of maintaining what Charles Aycock had called "good order" and of warding off federal intervention, an existential threat since the days of slavery.[27]

Challenging Jim Crow at School

A willingness to concede change at the margins shaped not only the battle over the ballot box but also the racial contest at the schoolhouse door. In the early 1930s, black educators, organized through the North Carolina Teachers Association (NCTA), collaborated with the NAACP in a campaign to equalize black and white teachers' pay. They were emboldened by the New Deal's support for organized labor and the minimum wage standards set by the National Recovery Administration. In October 1933, more than 2,500 teachers gathered in Raleigh to press their demands. Weeks later, their representatives issued a bold indictment of Jim Crow:

> We are disenfranchised and told to acquire learning and fitness for citizenship. We undertake the preparation in our inadequate, wretchedly equipped schools. Our children drag through the mud while others ride in buses, we pass the courses required by the state and in most places when we present ourselves for registration we are denied that right and lose our votes. Our teachers, disadvantaged by disenfranchisement, by lack of the means to prepare themselves, nevertheless do meet the high and exacting standards of the best white institutions of the country, and then armed with the state's highest

certificate go into the employment of a commonwealth which reduces their wages to the level of janitors and hod carriers.

The NCTA urged its members to register to vote and "unite their forces at the polls." "We are informed that it is best for us if we stay out of politics," the black educators declared, but "we have stayed out and this is what we have."[28]

That effort at political mobilization produced one of the South's earliest lawsuits to challenge the constitutionality of the literacy test. In 1934, two Iredell County teachers, T. E. Allison and Robert W. Dockery, appeared before a white registrar who instructed them to read and write passages from the state constitution. When they were done, he declared his judgment: "You do not satisfy me." Allison and Dockery subsequently sued the registrar and the county and state boards of elections.[29]

The North Carolina Supreme Court heard their case on appeal in 1936 and ruled for the defendants. Associate Justice R. Heriot Clarkson—a Confederate veteran and leader in the 1899 "White Supremacy Legislature"—wrote for the court. He affirmed the constitutionality of the literacy test and said of the plaintiffs, they "just do not like the law of their State." Clarkson closed with a history lesson: "It would not be amiss to say that [the] constitutional amendment providing for an educational test ... brought light out of darkness as to education for all the people of the State. Religious, educational, and material uplift went forward by leaps and bounds. . . . The rich and poor, the white and colored, alike have an equal . . . opportunity for an elementary and high school education."[30]

Given the difficulties of voter registration, the NCTA had limited ability to bring direct pressure to bear on state and local politicians, but its continued agitation of the salary equalization issue, the ongoing involvement of the NAACP, and a growing number of lawsuits filed elsewhere across the South convinced the state legislature in 1939 to allocate $250,000 to raise black teachers' pay. Still, the average black teacher earned only three-quarters of the average white teacher's compensation.[31]

The U.S. Court of Appeals for the Fourth Circuit put southern lawmakers on notice in 1940, when it ruled in a Norfolk, Virginia, case that racial disparities in teacher pay violated the equal protection clause of the Fourteenth Amendment. A three-judge panel affirmed black teachers' "civil right ... to pursue their profession without being subjected to discriminatory legislation on account of race or color." America's entry into World War II then provided the final impetus to close the gap. In 1942, James W. Seabrook, president of both the NCTA and Fayetteville State Teachers College (today, Fayetteville State University), appealed to white politicians' sense of fair play and their not-so-secret fears regarding black loyalty in the war effort. He urged them to "give the Negro confidence that the principles of democracy for which he is being called upon to fight in the four corners of the earth will be applied to him here at home." Two years later, the General Assembly appropriated the funds to equalize black and white teachers' salaries.[32]

During the war years, black educators' demand for equal pay expanded into a call for equal facilities. Children led the way. In October 1946, more than four hundred students, organized in a local NAACP Youth Council, filled the streets in Lumberton, a small town in southeastern North Carolina. They carried placards that cheered the triumph of democracy in World War II and set that achievement against the wretched condition of black schools: "inadequate and unhealthy . . . overcrowded . . . and dilapidated." "D-Day" and "V for Victory," the signs exclaimed. "How Can I Learn When I'm Cold?" "It Rains on Me." "Down with Our School."[33]

Protests spread across eastern and central North Carolina, accompanied by lawsuits that challenged the constitutionality of unequal school funding. In 1951, plaintiffs in Durham won a breakthrough case in the U.S. District Court for the Middle District of North Carolina. Justice Johnson Jay Hayes, a native of Wilkes County in the western part of the state, ruled that city officials had a legal obligation to provide "negro school children substantially equal facilities to those furnished white children." He found no "excuse or justification" for failing to meet that standard and ordered an end to discriminatory school spending.[34]

Anyone who read judge Hayes's ruling closely would have spotted a single sentence that was even more ominous in its implications. "The burdens inherent in segregation," he wrote, "must be met by the state which maintains" them. Had Hayes pronounced a death sentence for Jim Crow? In 1951, a group of fifty-five black parents filed suit in Pamlico County to test that question. They demanded that their children be assigned to white schools unless adequate black facilities were provided. As historian Sarah Thuesen has noted, this was "the first lawsuit filed in the federal courts from North Carolina—and only the second in the South—to raise the possibility of integration." The plaintiffs dropped their suit when the county agreed to build a new black high school, but they had made their point. As the editor of the Kinston *Free Press* noted, "If we want to keep segregation, we must bend over backward to see that facilities are equal."[35]

To that end, state leaders put a $50 million school bond on the ballot in late 1953, as the U.S. Supreme Court prepared to hear final arguments in *Brown v. Board*. One observer noted that many white voters supported the measure in the hope that it "might tend to influence" a judgment favorable to the South. They could not have been more mistaken. On May 17, 1954, the court ruled that "in the field of public education, the doctrine of 'separate but equal' has no place. Separate educational facilities are inherently unequal. Therefore, we hold that . . . segregation is a denial of the equal protection of the laws." In the aftermath of that decision, state and local officials scrambled once more to invent means of defending the substance if not the letter of Jim Crow laws.[36]

Brown v. Board and the Pearsall Committees

Two gubernatorial advisory committees, popularly known by the name of their chairman, wealthy eastern landowner and Democratic power broker Thomas J. Pearsall, set the course for opposition to *Brown*. They worked from the principle "that members of each race prefer to associate with other members of their race *and that they will do so naturally unless they are prodded and inflamed and controlled by outside pressure* [emphasis in the original]." To that end, the committees proposed "the building of a new school system on a new foundation—a foundation of no racial segregation by law, but assignment according to natural racial preference and the administrative determination of what is best for the child."[37]

The first Pearsall Committee recommended that the state cede authority over school assignments to local districts. That proposal informed the Pupil Assignment Act of 1955, passed in the same legislative session as the prohibition of single-shot voting. Lawmakers removed references to race from state school assignment policy and gave parents "freedom of choice" in selecting the schools their children would attend. But there was a catch. The law required that parents petition individually to have their children assigned to a school outside their neighborhood. Doing so demanded great courage. Black parents faced the prospect of retribution by angry employers and landlords, and they had to accept the risk that their children might stand alone to face white resistance. The law also gave local school boards broad discretionary authority in ruling on parents' requests. They could reject an application if they believed that it did not serve a child's "best interests" or would compromise "proper administration," "proper instruction," or "health or safety" in a target school.[38]

A year later, the second Pearsall Committee proposed an amendment to the state constitution that would authorize the legislature to provide private school vouchers for "any child assigned against the wishes of his parents to a school in which the races are mixed." Local school boards would also be permitted to call for public referenda to close schools in case of "enforced mixing of the races." The committee presented the amendment as a balm for racial conflict stirred up by so-called outsiders, most notably the NAACP and the federal courts. They looked forward to a day "when sanity returns," and to reestablishment of "the harmonious relations which the races have enjoyed in North Carolina for more than fifty years"—that is, from the time of white redemption and black disenfranchisement. In September 1956, voters approved the amendment by a margin of more than four to one. Though no schools were closed and only one private school voucher was issued, the amendment effectively undermined any notion that desegregation might be accomplished more quickly.[39]

These policies won North Carolina praise as a "moderate" southern state but produced one of the lowest desegregation rates in the region. At the beginning of the 1958–59 school year, only 10 of the state's roughly 322,000 black students were enrolled in formerly all-white schools. That result impressed a school official in Little Rock, Arkansas, where white resistance to desegregation had prompted President Dwight Eisenhower to use federal troops to restore order. He complimented his North Carolina colleagues: "You . . . have devised one of the cleverest techniques of perpetuating segregation that we have seen. . . . If we could be half as successful as you have been, we could keep this thing to a minimum for the next fifty years."[40]

The Little Rock admirer put his finger on a lesson that is as true today as it was in the 1950s. White supremacy, often violent and inflexible, can also be subtle and adaptive. A tobacco worker from eastern North Carolina said it best: "My experience . . . is that if you beat the white man at one trick, he will try another." That was the North Carolina way, and at the end of the 1950s, it appeared to be the most effective means of defending Jim Crow's regime.[41]

Chapter 4 Jim Crow's Demise

In 1960, black North Carolinians put whites on notice that they had no intention of enduring another half century of second-class citizenship. On February 1, Ezell Blair Jr., David Richmond, Franklin McCain, and Joseph McNeil—first-year students at the Agricultural and Technical College of North Carolina—made small purchases at the Woolworth's in downtown Greensboro and then, receipts in hand, sat down at the store's lunch counter and demanded service alongside white customers. Within days, they were joined by black women from Greensboro's Bennett College and white students from the city's University of North Carolina campus. Young people in Winston-Salem, Charlotte, Durham, and Raleigh quickly followed suit, and by the end of the month, sit-ins had spread to nearly every southern state.

In April, sit-in leaders from across the region gathered at Shaw University in Raleigh, the state's oldest black institution of higher education. Guided by Ella Baker, a Shaw graduate and field agent for Martin Luther King's Southern Christian Leadership Conference (SCLC), they founded the Student Nonviolent Coordinating Committee (SNCC), a radical new force that used grassroots organizing to create change from below. SNCC sent an army of young volunteers into communities across the South, where they organized direct-action protests, boycotts, and voter registration drives. Other civil rights organizations—including the NAACP, the SCLC, and the Congress on Racial Equality—joined the effort.

This uprising altered the course of the civil rights struggle. It took the battle to the streets and signaled, as historian William Chafe has observed, that "the terms of change would no longer be dictated by white southerners." Within five years, Jim Crow—at least as a system of laws—would be no more.[1]

The demise of Jim Crow's regime brought blacks and poor whites, who had been disenfranchised in 1900, back into the political system. It made room for restoration of the social vision that the triumph of white supremacy had driven underground, and accelerated the political realignment that had begun with the New Deal. That process was tumultuous, its trajectory sometimes easier to discern in hindsight than in the moment. A conservative vision of the sort that had dominated North Carolina politics through much of its history remained intact, though now embodied in the Republican Party. And the ideals that animated Republicanism in the 1860s and Fusion in the 1890s found new life among Democrats. History did not repeat itself, but it did, in fact, rhyme.

"To Give All Men and Women Their Best Chance in Life"

The 1960 Democratic gubernatorial primary marked a pivotal moment in this social and political transformation. In many respects, it resembled the 1950 senatorial contest between Willis Smith and Frank Graham. Four candidates vied for the nomination, only two of whom were serious contenders: I. Beverly Lake Sr. and Terry Sanford. Like Smith and Graham, they offered sharply opposed visions for North Carolina's future.

Lake was a respected jurist who had taught law at Wake Forest College and was widely admired among conservatives for his defense of Jim Crow. As state assistant attorney general during the mid-1950s, he prepared and presented a brief that shaped the U.S. Supreme Court's ruling on implementation of its 1954 *Brown* decision. Lake urged the court to "allow the greatest possible latitude to . . . District Judges in drafting final [desegregation] decrees." It stood to reason, he argued, that "only a court conversant with local conditions and granted wide discretion" could tailor a judgment to fit "local variations." Lake also offered a dire warning against any "attempt to compel the intermixture of the races." Such action would result in "violent opposition," he claimed, and place the public schools in "grave danger of destruction." In its 1955 ruling in *Brown II*, the high court heeded Lake's advice. The justices left it to lower courts to determine the pace and process of desegregation, guided by "their proximity to local conditions" and their understanding of the need for "practical flexibility in shaping remedies." That was the essence of *Brown II*'s directive that desegregation proceed "with all deliberate speed."[2]

By any estimation, Lake's performance before the Court was an astounding success, but he was not personally satisfied. Lake adamantly opposed school desegregation, whatever its speed. After his triumph in Washington, he proposed a plan to abandon North Carolina's public schools to blacks and organize local nonprofit corporations to run private schools for whites. In the 1960 gubernatorial campaign, Lake touted his devotion to white supremacy and the legacy of 1898 and 1900. On the stump and in newspaper advertisements, he echoed a fiery speech on *Brown* that he had delivered to the North Carolina Bar Association. "If we must choose between a generation of inferior education and the amalgamation of our races into a mixed-blooded whole," he warned, "let us choose inferior education since that is an evil which another generation can correct, while miscegenation is a tragedy which can never be undone." Lake assured white voters that they could stand by such bigotry in good conscience: "The PRINCIPLES for which we fight are ETERNAL!"[3]

Terry Sanford was a different breed of politician. Born in 1917, he was eleven years younger than Lake. He earned an undergraduate degree at the University of North Carolina in 1939, served as an army paratrooper in World War II, and then returned to Chapel Hill to study law. Sanford quickly became active in the Democratic Party. He volunteered in both Kerr Scott's and Frank Graham's campaigns and served in the state senate from 1953 to 1955. In February 1960, he announced a decision that he had been contemplating since his student days: he would be a candidate for governor.[4]

Sanford presented himself as a spokesman for voters of his generation who had come out of wartime with great confidence, an eagerness to escape the past, and a determination to create new lives for themselves and their children. "The time has come to quit holding back," he told a hometown crowd in Fayetteville. "I call on you to join with me to build a better North Carolina [that] is expanding, growing, developing." That appeal drew inspiration from a broad spirit of boosterism among business and civic leaders who were determined to modernize the state and integrate it fully into the national economy. They had begun in 1947 with a Good Health Campaign to fund the construction of local hospitals and to establish a four-year medical school on the university campus in Chapel Hill. During the following decade, state and local leaders also scoured the nation and the globe to attract $1 billion worth of new industrial development. That effort culminated in 1959 with the founding of the Research Triangle Park, which was designed to make the state a player in new fields of scientific research and technological innovation.[5]

In his bid for the governorship, Lake largely ignored such issues. The preservation of Jim Crow was his key policy concern, and at every turn he challenged Sanford for refusing to declare allegiance to white su-

IF YOU REALLY KNOW ...
Dr. BEVERLY LAKE
YOU'LL VOTE FOR HIM ON MAY 28

This Is The Man North Carolina Needs As Her

Governor

He Is "The Man Who Lets You Know

Where HE Stands"

AGRICULTURE BASIC TO ECONOMY

Dr. Lake supports the work of our Federal, State and Local agricultural leaders.

"I shall seek the advice of farm organizations and the Department of Agriculture."

"The problem of the small farmer is the most crucial issue facing North Carolina agriculture and we must work to help the small farmer because he is the backbone of our economy."

I. BEVERLY LAKE

BALANCED BUDGET NECESSARY—

Dr. Lake favors a balanced State budget; he is opposed to deficit State spending; and is strongly against raising our already burdensome taxes for desirable but non-essential improvements.

Dr. Lake proposes a "Policy of spending for current operating expenses no more than can be produced by fair tax laws not unduly burdensome".

SCHOOL INTEGRATION OPPOSED—

Dr. Lake is opposed to the mixing of white and Negro children in the schools in North Carolina.

"The mixing of our two great races in the classroom and then in the home is not inevitable and is not to be tolerated."

COURT AND HIGHWAY
CHANGES NEEDED—

Dr. Lake favors certain reforms in our court system directed toward a uniform, more efficient, and less costly system of justice for our people.

"Dr. Lake favors election of all judges, Recorders and Justice of Peace, by the people and is against proposals which would eliminate this plan."

"I favor a highway commission of fourteen members, one appointed from each of the 14 engineering divisions."

Political Adv Paid for by Perquimans Lake For Governor Committee

I. Beverly Lake campaign ad. *Perquimans Weekly* (Hertford, N.C.), May 27, 1960.

"The PRINCIPLES for which we fight are ETERNAL!"

I. Beverly Lake

I. Beverly Lake campaign card, 1960. Courtesy of the Lew Powell Memorabilia Collection, North Carolina Collection, Wilson Library, University of North Carolina at Chapel Hill.

premacy. Sanford would not be baited. As a young politician active in Frank Graham's campaign, he had learned the danger of allowing an opponent to make race the issue. He also admired Kerr Scott's skill at deflection. When Lake attacked, Sanford pivoted to the "bright look of the future" and invited voters to join him in building for a "New Day" in North Carolina. He spoke of improving rather than closing public schools. "We are going to continue to go forward," Sanford declared, "to give our children a better chance, to build a better state through better schools." That appeal was reassuring and persuasive, particularly for young white women, who worried about their children's future and volunteered in droves for Sanford's campaign.[6]

On Election Day, Sanford won 41.3 percent of the votes. The three other candidates, with Lake at the head, split the rest. Because Sanford failed to secure a majority, Lake was entitled to a runoff in June. Black leaders saw the sharp contrast between the two candidates as an opportunity to make the second primary a referendum on Jim Crow. In a Democratic Party in which whites were split almost evenly between those who remained faithful to the principles of Charles Aycock and Josiah Bailey and those who supported Kerr Scott and Frank Graham, even a small number of registered black voters had the power to determine the outcome of a critical election. Admittedly, Sanford was not an ideal civil rights candidate. He had supported the work of the Pearsall committees and had at times been highly critical of the NAACP, but he was also open-minded and educable. Kelly Alexander, president of the state conference of the NAACP, viewed Sanford as a candidate who would approach "the race question" with "wisdom and understanding." Across North Carolina, black business and civic leaders raised money for Sanford's campaign, and on Election Day, black voters turned out at the polls. Sanford defeated Lake by 76,000 votes—a number that fit neatly into estimates that between 63,000 and 81,000 blacks cast their ballots for him. Louis Austin's *Carolina Times* crowed, "Negro Vote Sanford's Win Margin."[7]

Sanford took office with little to say about the civil rights struggle that was roiling around him, but black North Carolinians quickly began to instruct him. Some of his most persuasive teachers were the black children he met in 1962 on a statewide tour of public schools. Sanford looked to education as a cure-all for North Carolina's ills, including the injustices inflicted by Jim Crow. He pushed a new sales tax through the legislature in order to expand investment in public education and em-

Governor Terry Sanford visits students at Merrick-Moore Elementary School, Durham, 1962. Courtesy of the State Archives of North Carolina, Raymond Stone Photograph Collection of Governor Terry Sanford's Education Tour, 1962.

barked on a school tour to spotlight the difference more money could make. "I told students," he later recalled, "that this is not the age for the common laborer; you must have a skill and you must work here and now to get it. Education is your future." But when he looked black children in the eye, the governor had "a sickening feeling" that he was "saying words that were a mockery" to them, that at a tender age they were already caught up in a "cycle of tragedy." The "improvement of schools wasn't enough," Sanford concluded. "Not nearly enough."[8]

When Sanford was at home in the governor's mansion in Raleigh, black protesters in the streets reinforced that lesson. They were part of the sit-in movement that had erupted in Greensboro just days before he announced his candidacy and had spread throughout the state and across the South. Young people, black and white, put their bodies on the line to declare that they, not the defenders of Jim Crow, would set the pace of change and that there would be no turning back. Four months after Sanford's inauguration, the firebombing of a Freedom Riders bus outside Anniston, Alabama, made it clear that white resistance to black gains would exact a horrific human price.

In the privacy of his office, a small circle of black advisers Sanford had cultivated during the 1960 campaign urged him to come to grips with these issues before it was too late. John Hervey Wheeler, president of Durham's black-owned Mechanics and Farmers Bank, issued a stern warning with which others concurred: all that the governor hoped to accomplish for the state was on the line. "North Carolina," Wheeler insisted, "cannot enjoy the bright sunshine of a New Day in industry, agriculture, education, and democratic living unless it frees each one of its citizens to develop to the maximum of his capabilities."[9]

Sanford took all of these lessons to heart. By late 1962, he was feeling a sense of urgency. "I knew," he later recalled, "that I had to make a firmer determination of where we were headed." In November, Sanford reminded a meeting of the Southern Association of Colleges and Schools that the end of slavery had opened up new opportunities for the South—opportunities that white elites had squandered with the imposition of Jim Crow. He urged his white audience to get it right this time. The South needed a new "Emancipation Proclamation," Sanford argued, "[one] which will set us free to grow and build, set us free from the drag of poor people, poor schools, from hate and demagoguery. It has to be a bold dream for the future, realistic in terms of our country, and aware that the South is entering the mainstream of American life. . . . The South, and the rest of the nation for that matter, needs to take a long, hard look at itself to see where it stands now and to see where it hopes to stand twenty years from now." Implicit in that admonition was an acknowledgment of the common fate of all southerners, black and white, rich and poor.[10]

At every turn, black advisers pressed Sanford not to compromise his message. In early January 1963, the governor invited a small group of confidantes, including several black businessmen and professionals, to a breakfast meeting at his residence. He wanted to share notes for another speech he was preparing on "Negro rights" and the South's future. He had titled it "Observations for a Second Century." When John Wheeler read the notes, he immediately objected that their tone was too moderate. He urged Sanford to focus on economic and political change rather than appeal for "goodwill" between the races. Others in the room, particularly a number of conservative Democratic Party leaders, disagreed, and a heated discussion ensued. In the end, Wheeler prevailed.[11]

On January 18, Sanford traveled to Chapel Hill to deliver a revised version of his address at the annual meeting of the North Carolina Press Association. He began with a personal aside to men and women he knew well and respected as opinion makers: "I wanted to take this occasion, talking to [you] to say something . . . that I have long wanted to say, that I believe we must say." Then he read his prepared statement, which took its cue from the one hundredth anniversary of Emancipation on January 1, 1863. He beseeched the journalists to join him in a campaign to make good on America's unfulfilled promise of freedom and equality:

> The American Negro was freed from slavery one hundred years ago. In this century, he has made much progress, educating his children, building churches, entering into the community and civic life of the nation.
>
> Now is the time in this hundredth year not merely to look back to freedom but forward to the fulfillment of its meaning. Despite this great progress, the Negro's opportunity to obtain a good job has not been achieved in most places across the nation. Reluctance to accept the Negro in employment is the greatest single block to his continued progress and to the full use of the human potential of the nation and its states.
>
> The time has come for American citizens to give up this reluctance, to quit unfair discrimination, and to give the Negro a full chance to earn a decent living for his family and to contribute to higher standards for himself and all men.
>
> North Carolina and its people have come to the point of recognizing the urgent need for opening new economic opportunities for Negro citizens. We also recognize that in doing so we shall be adding new economic growth for everybody.
>
> We can do this. We should do this. We will do it because we are concerned with the problems and the welfare of our neighbors. We will do it because our economy cannot afford to have so many people fully and partially unproductive. We will do it because it is honest and fair for us to give all men and women their best chance in life.

As he spoke to the journalists, Sanford must have been mindful of another southern governor who had been in the headlines just four days earlier. In his inaugural address, delivered from the steps of the state capitol in Montgomery, Alabama, George C. Wallace exclaimed, "Segregation now, segregation tomorrow, and segregation forever."[12] Sanford may also have had Wallace on his mind three months later, when he traveled to the Agricultural and Technical College of North Carolina in Greensboro to receive the Omega Psi Phi Fraternity's Citizen of the Year Award. Standing before an all-black student audience, he called for an end to racial segregation. "We must move forward as one people or we will not move forward at all," Sanford declared. "We cannot move forward as whites or Negroes. . . . We can only move forward as North Carolinians." Those words refuted the defining principle of a white man's democracy, which Charles Aycock had explained in 1901 to an audience at the Negro State Fair in Raleigh. "It is absolutely necessary that each race should remain distinct," Aycock said, "and have a society of its own. . . . The law which separates you from the white people of the State . . . always has been and always will be inexorable." Sanford knew better, because black North Carolinians had taught him to understand the destructive consequences of that supposedly "eternal" truth.[13]

Lifting the Economic Burden of Jim Crow

To defeat Jim Crow, Terry Sanford declared war on poverty. Racial segregation and the low-wage economy it sustained inflicted hardship and suffering on millions of North Carolinians. In 1960, 37 percent of the state's residents—twice the national average—lived below the poverty line, and in eastern counties, where sharecropping had taken the place of plantation slavery, black impoverishment was so deep and pervasive that outsiders referred to the region as "North Carolina's 'little Mississippi.'" For Democratic Party leaders in the General Assembly, most of whom came from the east, these facts gave little cause for alarm. The lawmakers were far more concerned with squelching civil rights protests and protecting the conservative principles that animated Jim Crow's regime and defined their own economic interests: small government, cheap labor, low taxation, and limited spending on all forms of social provision.[14]

With little room to maneuver politically, Sanford sidestepped the legislature and partnered with private philanthropy to attack what he and his advisers came to call the "poverty-segregation complex." In the summer of 1963, he announced the establishment of the North Carolina Fund, a nongovernmental organization that would invest in experimental antipoverty programs at the community level. The fund was backed by $7 million from the Ford Foundation, plus another $2.5 million from the Z. Smith Reynolds and Mary Reynolds Babcock Foundations, both headquartered in Winston-Salem. Adjusted for inflation, those commitments would be valued at more than $80 million today. News of the fund garnered national attention. Indeed, aides to Lyndon B. Johnson looked to the North Carolina initiative as a model for the president's own war on poverty, which he launched with passage of the Economic Opportunity Act in 1964. In the years that followed, the North Carolina Fund became the pipeline for millions of dollars of antipoverty spending provided by the federal Office of Economic Opportunity and the Departments of Housing and Urban Development, Labor, and Health, Education, and Welfare.[15]

The fund focused its efforts on eleven community-based projects—four in the east, four in the Piedmont, and another three in the western mountains—that had been proposed by groups of civic and religious leaders, politicians, and concerned citizens. Each project was led by a community-action agency that was organized at the local level and financed by the fund. Initially, the agencies relied heavily on college students the fund recruited and trained as North Carolina Volunteers. Those young people lived and worked in interracial teams with an explicit commitment to building relationships across lines of class and color. In their host communities, they tutored schoolchildren, taught adults to read and write, repaired dilapidated housing, built playgrounds, and organized recreation programs. As federal money began flowing, the community-action agencies hired staff, often out of the impoverished neighborhoods they served, and took on larger initiatives. They ran job training for high school dropouts, started early childhood education programs, constructed water systems in rural areas, organized impoverished urban neighborhoods to demand paved streets and sanitation services, and guided families in need of food and clothing through the often intimidating process of applying for public assistance.[16]

As the fund and its partners took up this war on poverty, they encountered stiff resistance. Many local leaders had embraced the fund because of the financial resources it promised to deliver to their communities, but they were not prepared to upset established structures of authority, power, and privilege. In the western counties of Watauga, Avery, Mitchell, and Yancey, politicians killed plans for a poor people's newspaper on grounds that the project was a communistic enterprise that would invite federal meddling in local affairs. In the northeast, officials in Northampton, Halifax, Hertford, and Bertie Counties refused to operate racially integrated Head Start centers, and by doing so risked the loss of federal funds meant to benefit 2,300 low-income children. Across the state, threats of violence accompanied the fund's work. In New Bern, night riders shot up the house in which student volunteers were living; Klansmen stalked others on the campus of Livingstone College, a black institution in Salisbury; and in Coats, a small railroad town in Harnett County, the Klan threatened to burn down a building that fund workers had converted into an integrated library for children.[17]

While whites defended the established order at home, their senators in Washington—Samuel (Sam) J. Ervin Jr. and B. Everett Jordan— battled against passage of the Civil Rights Act of 1964. Ervin, in fact, was "one of the strategists" in the effort, on account of his mastery of parliamentary procedure. He and other southerners filibustered for sixty days to stop a bill that they characterized as a "debasement of constitutional government and an exaltation of governmental tyranny." They believed that it threatened, as Ervin would later say of all civil rights legislation, to "steal freedom from one man to confer it on another."[18]

A coalition of Republicans and liberal Democrats (all but one of whom were from outside the South) finally broke the filibuster in June, and Lyndon Johnson signed the Civil Rights Act of 1964 into law in July. The law barred discrimination on the basis of race, color, religion, or national origin in public schools, public accommodations (such as hotels, theaters, and restaurants), and public facilities (such as parks, sports arenas, and libraries). It also included women in its protection of equal employment opportunities, expanded the mandate of the Civil Rights Commission established in 1957, and authorized federal agencies to withhold funds from programs and activities that violated these guarantees.[19]

There was a clear political lesson in these struggles of the early 1960s. Jim Crow had ruled for more than half a century, and the beneficiaries of that regime wielded tremendous clout in the halls of government. As one North Carolina Fund staffer explained, "Not a whole lot was going to change . . . without changing [the structure] of power." Realizing that this could not be accomplished without guaranteeing every citizen free and fair access to the ballot box, voting rights advocates had pushed to include strong protections in the Civil Rights Act of 1964, but President Johnson and congressional leaders feared that doing so would jeopardize the bill. As a result, the most significant voting provisions in the law simply required that literacy tests be standardized and administered equitably.[20]

Shortly after passage of the civil rights legislation, Johnson instructed the Justice Department to prepare "the god-damnedest, toughest voting rights act that you can devise." He wanted to have a bill in hand after the upcoming November election, on the assumption that he would then be better positioned to push it through Congress. In the meantime, civil rights activists kept the pressure on. One of the most visible efforts was SNCC's 1964 Freedom Summer campaign. The organization sent more than one thousand college volunteers, mostly white and mostly from the North, into rural Mississippi to run "freedom schools" for black children and to register adults to vote. Local whites answered with frightful violence. In late June, KKK members, in coordination with local law enforcement in Neshoba County, ambushed and murdered three civil rights workers: James Chaney, Andrew Goodman, and Michael Schwerner. Many Americans were horrified by television and newspaper reports when the FBI discovered their bodies buried in an earthen dam.[21]

Months later, local activists, SNCC workers, and Martin Luther King Jr.'s Southern Christian Leadership Conference launched a voting rights campaign in Selma, Alabama, and surrounding counties. As in Mississippi, violence quickly ensued. In February, an Alabama state trooper shot and killed Jimmie Lee Jackson, an army veteran and Baptist deacon, during a voting rights demonstration in the small town of Marion. The following month—on March 7, the day that became known as Bloody Sunday—protestors attempted to walk from Selma to the state capitol in Montgomery, fifty-three miles away, to honor Jackson's sacrifice and demand the right to register and vote. State troopers and newly deputized posse men, some on horseback, stopped the procession on the Edmund Pettus Bridge, named for a Confederate general and Grand Dragon of the Alabama Klan. The lawmen teargassed and mercilessly beat the marchers. Televised images of the confrontation were broadcast across the nation and around the world. Eight days later, President Johnson—"moved," he said, by "the cries of pain and the hymns and protests of oppressed people"—addressed a joint session of Congress to demand speedy passage of legislation to "strike down restrictions to voting in all elections—Federal, State, and local."[22]

Johnson called white Americans to task for their century-long refusal to make good on the promise of equal citizenship. He reminded members of Congress and a national television audience that Americans' most treasured right was "the right to choose [their] own leaders" and that the measure of the country's progress was the "expansion of that right to all of our people." "Every American citizen must have an equal right to vote," Johnson declared. He also refuted opponents' all-too-familiar objections. "There is no constitutional issue here," he avowed. "The command of the Constitution is plain. There is no moral issue here. It is wrong—deadly wrong—to deny any of your fellow Americans the right to vote in this country. There is no issue of States' rights or national rights. There is only the struggle for human rights."[23]

In a line that surely startled many white lawmakers and television viewers, Johnson insisted that "the real hero of this struggle is the American Negro," whose "persistent bravery and . . . faith in American democracy" had brought the nation to a moment of reckoning. And in so doing, the black freedom struggle promised to liberate millions more from poverty, hunger, and homelessness. In words that echoed past efforts to build an inclusive democracy, Johnson asked that his audience reflect on the collateral damage done by Jim Crow: "How many white children have gone uneducated," he asked, "how many white families have lived in stark poverty, how many white lives have been scarred by fear, because we have wasted our energy and our substance to maintain the barriers of hatred?"[24]

Congress passed the Voting Rights Act of 1965 in early July, and President Johnson signed it into law on August 6. The law prohibited the use of literacy tests and required federal approval, or "preclearance," for changes to voting laws in jurisdictions where less than half of eligible citizens were registered to vote as of November 1, 1964, or less than half of eligible citizens voted in the 1964 presidential election. The preclearance provision originally applied to all of Mississippi, Louisiana, Alabama, Georgia, South Carolina, and Virginia, along with forty counties in North Carolina, all but thirteen of which were in the east.[25]

Passage of the Voting Rights Act answered the question much on the minds of North Carolina Fund staff: How could they reorganize the structure of power? Beginning in late 1965, they steered the agency in a new direction. The fund moved away from serving people in poverty to organizing them politically, getting them out to vote, and mobilizing them to demand fair treatment by government officials, landlords, and employers. This effort to create what fund staff referred to as an army of the "organized and articulate poor" gained its strongest foothold in two locations: the Piedmont tobacco and textile manufacturing city of Durham and the rural counties in the northeastern corner of the state.

Both were home to black communities with long traditions of independent political activity.[26]

In Durham, the North Carolina Fund pulled together a confederation of neighborhood councils called United Organizations for Community Improvement (UOCI), which had its own board of directors elected from the ranks of the poor. That board set priorities and allocated financial resources channeled through the fund. The UOCI used the money to organize rent strikes against Durham's most notorious slumlords, create a tenants' council among residents of public housing, demand better wages for support staff in the city's public schools, and press officials to pave the streets and pick up the trash in low-income neighborhoods. Through these efforts, members of the neighborhood councils came to understand that making change required an incursion into party politics. They began attending Democratic precinct meetings, and in some instances did so in large enough numbers to displace white power brokers. In 1968, the organized poor elected Ann Atwater—a forceful, outspoken leader of the neighborhood councils—as vice chair of the Durham County Democratic Party.[27]

The fund's work in the Choanoke region—Halifax, Northampton, Hertford, and Bertie Counties—followed a similar trajectory. There the fund financed the People's Program on Poverty (PPOP), an organization made up of more than three thousand black sharecroppers and domestic workers. The program focused on gaining access to public resources and creating opportunities for economic independence. Banks in the Choanoke region systematically denied credit to black borrowers; local governments refused to enforce—or often even to enact—housing codes; and while the federal government offered various forms of housing assistance, local administrators routinely withheld information from black residents. The Reverend James A. Felton, a U.S. Marines veteran and PPOP founder, made these issues his special concern. He developed an expert knowledge of federal housing policy, traveled to Washington to visit officials, and organized workshops for PPOP members. As a result, more than one hundred families applied to the Farmers Home Administration for low-interest loans, and fourteen communities secured grants from the same agency to build neighborhood water systems that replaced shallow, often polluted wells. PPOP also established a rural cooperative to help blacks farm independently and a worker-owned sewing company that made uniforms and parachutes for the military. Like most whites, a local television news re-

Ann Atwater canvasses for votes in Durham. Courtesy of the Billy Ebert Barnes Collection, North Carolina Collection, Wilson Library, University of North Carolina at Chapel Hill.

porter saw in these declarations of black citizenship and self-reliance little more than "heaped up, packed down and running over hatred for the white race."[28]

Elsewhere in North Carolina, the fund joined forces with the Voter Education Project (VEP), which had been established in 1962 by the Southern Regional Council, a liberal interracial organization. The VEP, like the fund, was backed by private philanthropy. Since its founding, it had worked on voter registration in partnership with local and national civil rights organizations. In early 1967, the fund and the VEP launched a North Carolina Voter Education Project. For legal and tactical reasons, the initiative was officially nonpartisan, but when speaking among themselves, its organizers were clear about their purpose. They aimed to build a biracial political alliance of "poor and disadvantaged" citizens that would make the state Democratic Party into an instrument of social and political reconstruction.[29]

The North Carolina VEP pursued that goal through registration drives, precinct-level leadership training, and voter education programs, including the distribution of instructional pamphlets for people who had never voted. These aids used words and pictures to teach about state and local government and to walk new voters through the election process, from registering to finding the proper polling place, filling out a ballot, and dealing with officials who might question voters' qualifications. In its first year alone, the North Carolina VEP sponsored five registration drives and added more than 7,000 voters to the rolls, including 4,500 in Robeson County, where canvassers visited black and Lumbee Indian residents in their homes.[30]

Ghosts of Jim Crow

With passage of the Civil Rights Act of 1964 and the Voting Rights Act of 1965, Jim Crow's regime—at least as a legal entity—was dead. The situation in the South in many ways resembled the post–Civil War years. The federal government had legislated racial equality, but like their brethren a century before, conservatives in the 1960s had no intention of surrendering their power and privilege. In the state legislature, they fought a determined battle to limit additional black gains and to assure white constituents that Democrats would not become the "Negro party." They were remarkably creative in their efforts and initially had some success. But by the mid-1980s, conservatives were running out of options. Black North Carolinians had the law and the courts on their side, and they were gaining influence within the Democratic Party. Under those circumstances, a growing number of whites began to look for a new political home.[31]

The first skirmish concerned article 2 of North Carolina's constitution, which guaranteed every county a seat in the state house of representatives. In the twentieth century, as the state industrialized and cities grew, that provision disadvantaged urban counties with large and rapidly growing black populations and privileged less densely populated rural counties—many of them in the east, where whites were most firmly in control. By the mid-1960s, the district with the largest population had nearly twenty times more residents than the district with the smallest. That meant that a majority in the house "could be assembled from members who represented only 27.09 percent of the state's [total] population." The state senate was apportioned more evenly. The constitution required that senate districts contain equal populations, though a separate provision that no county was to be divided did create some imbalance. The largest senate districts had nearly three times more residents than the smallest.[32]

In 1965, Renn Drum Jr., a Winston-Salem attorney, sued in federal court, claiming that North Carolina's method of apportioning legislative seats violated the principle of "one man, one vote." The U.S. Supreme Court had established that standard in a series of rulings earlier in the decade that required equality of population across electoral districts. The court's concern was to ensure that every vote cast would have equal value in determining an election's outcome. In November, the U.S. District Court for the Middle District of North Carolina ruled in Drum's favor. A three-judge panel concluded that the state's practice of apportioning legislative seats on the basis of geography rather than population was "in violation of the Equal Protection provisions of the Fourteenth Amendment." They directed the General Assembly to "rectify the inequities" identified in the case; otherwise, the court would impose its own "scheme of apportionment."[33]

Lawmakers met in special session in January 1966 to take up that work. They reduced population ratios as the court directed, but did so by creating a large number of multimember districts—fifteen of thirty-three in the senate, which previously had thirty-six districts, eleven of which were multimember; and forty-one of forty-nine in the house, which previously had one hundred districts, twelve of which were multimember. Initially, seats in all of the multimember districts were to be filled through at-large elections. This was a familiar means of disadvantaging black candidates. Lawmakers had used it effectively in the 1950s when they changed county and municipal governments from ward to at-large systems of representation.[34]

In 1967, lawmakers did two things that further walled off the General Assembly. First, they approved a constitutional amendment, ratified by voters in the next election, that required that counties be kept whole in the creation of state house as well as senate districts. This effectively made multimember districts a permanent feature of legislative apportionment. Without such a solution, it was mathematically impossible to respect county lines and at the same time base house and senate seats on equal measures of population.[35]

Second, lawmakers added a numbered-seat plan in twenty of the forty-one multimember house districts and three of the fifteen multimember districts in the senate. Taken together, these districts covered nearly all of the heavily black counties in the eastern section of the state. The apportionment law directed that in multimember districts each seat would be treated as a separate office. When citizens went to the polls, they would no longer vote for a set number of candidates out of a larger field of contenders—for instance, three out of five. Instead, their ballots would list separate races within the district, and they would vote for only one candidate in each race.[36]

Proponents explained that the numbered-seat scheme was designed to "cure the problem of 'single-shot' voting," which was still legal in legislative elections. With conservative Democrats' critique of black bloc voting clearly in mind, one lawmaker explained that in a numbered-seat election, "you are running against a man and not a group." Another added that numbered seats all but guaranteed "that no Negro could be elected to the General Assembly." The numbered-seat plan was, indeed, so effective that in 1971 the General Assembly had only two black members: Henry E. Frye, a lawyer from Guilford County, who was elected to his first term in 1968 through a single-shot campaign, and Joy J. Johnson, a minister from Robeson County, who ran in one of the few eastern districts without numbered seats. Frye was the first black lawmaker to be elected to the General Assembly since 1898.[37]

Lawmakers attempted to expand the scope of the numbered-seat plan in 1971. They reapportioned the lower chamber to have forty-five districts. Thirty-five were multimember, and of those, twenty-three had numbered seats. In the senate, there were twenty-seven districts. Eighteen were multimember, and within that group, eleven districts had numbered seats. Had these changes been implemented, the numbered-seat plan would have covered all North Carolina counties with populations that were 30 percent or more black. But the U.S. Department of Justice blocked the move. It did so under authority of section 5 of the Voting Rights Act, which stipulated that in affected jurisdictions, changes to voting and representation had to be precleared by either the U.S. attorney general or the U.S. District Court for the District of Columbia to ensure that they would not discriminate against protected minorities. In 1972, the U.S. District Court for the Eastern District of North Carolina affirmed the Justice Department's decision. Ruling in *Dunston v. Scott*, the court struck down both the numbered-seat plan and the anti-single-shot laws that regulated elections in certain counties and municipalities. A three-judge panel concluded that "selective and arbitrary application" of both provisions "in some districts and not in others, denies to the voters of North Carolina the equal protection of the laws and is unconstitutional."[38]

Though not a basis for their decision, the judges also suggested that the single-shot prohibition violated the U.S. Constitution by constraining voters' choice in their use of the ballot: "We are inclined to believe that the right to vote includes the right of the voter to refuse to vote for someone he does not know, may not agree with, or may believe to be a fool, and under the Fourteenth and Fifteenth Amendments, we doubt that the state may constitutionally compel a voter to vote for a candidate of another race or political philosophy in order to get his vote counted."[39]

In subsequent elections, black representation in the General Assembly grew from two members in 1970 to a high of six in both 1974 and 1976. The number then fell back to five in 1978 and to four in 1980. Numbered seats or not, black candidates were still hard-pressed to win in multimember districts.[40]

In 1981, four black voters filed suit in *Gingles v. Edmisten* to challenge the use of multimember districts in the legislative redistricting plan that the General Assembly had crafted after the 1980 census and the 1968 constitutional provision that counties not be divided when apportioning state house and senate seats. Lawmakers had not submitted the plan or the amendment for preclearance by the Justice Department; when they did so after the plaintiffs' filing, both were denied approval.[41]

Lawmakers reacted quickly by drafting a new plan that included five majority-black house districts and one majority-black senate district. The creation of those districts aided the election of eight new black members of the house, raising the total from three to eleven. As the court later noted, however, the legislature's change of heart was in some measure cynical. "The pendency of this very legislation," the court observed, "worked a one-time advantage for black candidates in the form of unusual organized political support by white leaders concerned to forestall single-member districting." The U.S. District Court for the Eastern District of North Carolina ruled for the *Gingles* plaintiffs in April 1984. Acting in an extra session, the General Assembly subsequently divided a number of multimember districts into new single-member districts that improved the prospects of black candidates. In November balloting, two additional black lawmakers were elected to the General Assembly, bringing the total to thirteen.[42]

By 1989, nineteen black lawmakers served in the General Assembly, then a record for any one legislative session in state history. Two years later, members elected Dan Blue Speaker of the House, to this day the highest office ever held by a black politician in North Carolina.

Blacks also made substantial gains at the local level, largely as a result of legal challenges to at-large elections and multimember districts that followed the *Gingles* decision. At the end of the decade, more than four hundred black elected officials served in county and municipal governments across the state.[43]

Growing black political influence was also evident in 1991, when the General Assembly redrew North Carolina's congressional districts on the basis of the 1990 census. Under pressure from the U.S. Department of Justice and black leaders in the Democratic Party, legislators created two districts with slim black majorities. They explained that had they not done so, the state would have been vulnerable to legal challenge for violating the Voting Rights Act of 1965. The issue was dilution of the black vote. In most parts of the state, the geographical scope of congressional districts submerged black voters in sizable white majorities. Statewide, whites also had a long, well-documented history of refusing to support black candidates. As a result, it was difficult for black voters to make their voices heard in federal elections. To remedy this marginalization, lawmakers created a new First Congressional District in the heavily black northeastern corner of the state and a new Twelfth District that snaked along a narrow, 160-mile path from Durham to Charlotte. In 1992, voters in these districts elected Eva Clayton and Mel Watt, the first black North Carolinians to serve in the U.S. House of Representatives since George Henry White, who ended his second term in 1901.[44]

A New White Man's Party

As black gains mounted, a growing number of white conservatives chose to abandon the Democratic Party rather than stand and fight within it. That process had begun in the 1964 presidential election. The Civil Rights Act figured prominently in that contest. Arizona senator Barry M. Goldwater, who had voted against the law, won the Republican nomination with near unanimous support from southern delegates at the party's national convention. He insisted throughout the campaign that he was neither a racist nor a segregationist, but instead opposed civil rights legislation on constitutional grounds. The federal government, he argued, did not have the authority to compel the states or individuals to comply with beliefs about racial equality that they did not share. That said, Goldwater was not shy about admitting the racially charged appeal of his ideas. In 1961, he had told a gathering of southern Republican leaders that the party should "stop trying to outbid the

Democrats for the Negro vote" and instead "go hunting where the ducks are." That advice echoed President Herbert Hoover's appeal to the white South during his administration and would come to be known as the Republican Party's "southern strategy."[45]

In a television address broadcast nationally in prime time, actor and former Democrat Ronald Reagan underscored Goldwater's message and positioned himself as a future leader of the conservative cause. Reagan opposed civil rights legislation and Lyndon Johnson's war on poverty and later built his political career around those issues. As governor of California, he promised to overturn fair housing legislation, arguing that "if an individual wants to discriminate against Negroes . . . he has a right to do so." In his first bid for the presidency in 1976, he rallied supporters with stories of "welfare queens" who stole from the public purse, and as president he opposed extension of the Voting Rights Act, noting that the original legislation had been "humiliating to the South." In his televised endorsement of Goldwater in 1964, Reagan wrapped such sentiments in Cold War fears of Soviet communism. He told voters that they faced a stark choice between "individual freedom," on the one hand, and, on the other, a downward path toward "centralized government" and "totalitarianism." In broadest terms, there was nothing new about this message. It had deep resonance with the case for southern secession in 1861 and the rationale for white America's twentieth-century embrace of Jim Crow.[46]

Johnson defeated Goldwater in a landslide, and in the aftermath of the election, many observers were quick to announce the death of conservatism. But Goldwater's showing below the Mason-Dixon Line suggested that they misread the moment. In addition to carrying his own state, the Arizonan won South Carolina, Georgia, Alabama, Mississippi, and Louisiana with totals ranging from 54 to 87 percent of the vote. In North Carolina, he won a remarkable 44 percent. These numbers were a harbinger of what was to come in state and national politics.[47]

Sim A. DeLapp, former chairman of the Republican Party in North Carolina, found hope in the number of whites who, despite being lifelong Democrats, were willing to vote for Goldwater. He believed that he understood their sense of grievance. "Right now," DeLapp declared, "we are being ruled by the minorities. The member of the majority is the forgotten man." There was opportunity here. DeLapp urged Republicans to study white Democrats' victory in 1898 to see how "members of the majority" might be persuaded to "rise up and turn against the minority groups." The key was to revitalize the Republican Party as a white man's party, and by doing so "use the race issue again to regain power."[48]

That would not be a difficult task. After 1900, the North Carolina Republican Party had limited political influence, except to express western counties' generations-old resentment toward the economic and political power of Piedmont and eastern interests. Beyond that, Republicans were not so different from Aycock Democrats. In the early years of Jim Crow, they purged their party of blacks and, by their own account, made it "Lily-White." They also opposed the expansion of federal power in Franklin Roosevelt's New Deal and Lyndon Johnson's war on poverty. For white Democrats who could get beyond what they had learned in school about Republicans and the "crimes" of Reconstruction, switching sides—once unthinkable—became imaginable.[49]

DeLapp and like-minded Republican leaders saw James C. Gardner, a young upstart from eastern North Carolina, as the person to spearhead the party's revitalization. Gardner was born in Nash County in 1933 and grew up on a large dairy farm outside Rocky Mount. He studied for two years at North Carolina State University and served in the army during the Korean War. In the early 1960s, he and a business partner bought the franchise rights for a hamburger stand in Greenville and quickly built the enterprise into Hardee's, one of the nation's leading fast-food chains. That success gave Gardner entrée into Rocky Mount's civic elite. He joined the Jaycees and moved easily among a close network of the city's bankers, lawyers, doctors, and business owners.[50]

Conversations within that group often turned to politics and concern for the "end to a way of life" in the South. The men and women in Gardner's circle differed in their views on what was to be done. Some remained loyal to the Democratic Party and tried to hold the line on black political participation, while others established a local chapter of the ultraconservative John Birch Society, a libertarian and fiercely anti-communist organization founded by North Carolina native and University of North Carolina alumnus Robert W. Welch Jr. Gardner cast his lot with a third clutch of friends who had left the Democratic Party and formed a Republican county committee. In 1963, he too changed his party affiliation.[51]

Gardner approached politics with an entrepreneur's eye. He recognized that there was an untapped market of white North Carolinians like himself who felt abandoned by the Democratic Party and did not know where to turn. Gardner meant to offer them a solution. In 1964, he attempted to unseat Fourth District congressman Harold D. Cooley, who had been in office since the Great Depression. In a calculated effort to win support from white Democrats, Gardner posted more than ninety billboards that made no mention of his party affiliation. They simply read, "Goldwater-Gardner: Conservatives." On the campaign trail, Gardner touted individual rights, called for an end to the coddling of civil rights protestors, and characterized the Civil Rights Act of 1964, then pending in Congress, as "nothing but a cover up for increased federal control." Gardner, like Goldwater, was defeated, but his ability to convince once-loyal Democrats to cross over and cast their ballots for him was impressive. He garnered 48 percent of the vote, slightly more than Goldwater. In the 1966 election, Gardner challenged Cooley again and won by a thirteen-point margin.[52]

As a new member of Congress, Gardner voiced his supporters' grievances and sought to make a name for himself by launching an attack on the North Carolina Fund and its connections to the civil rights movement. In press conferences and on the floor of the House of Representatives, he warned that in the eastern part of the state fund staff were promoting "'revolutionary . . . attitudes'" by speaking of the need for a "coalition . . . between poor whites and Negroes to give political power to the disadvantaged." This "dangerous situation," Gardner advised, was also smoldering in communities across the nation.[53]

Proof of that claim seemed close to hand during the summer of 1967, when Newark, New Jersey, and Detroit, Michigan, erupted in violence. In both places, episodes of police brutality unleashed torrents of rage among black residents who had been bottled up in segregated inner-city neighborhoods, where habitable housing, employment opportunities, and good schools were all in short supply. Newark burned for six days. By the time the National Guard restored order, the central city was in ruins and twenty-six residents—almost all of them black—had been killed. Less than a week later, an even deadlier conflict broke out in Detroit, much of it carried live on television. More than two thousand buildings went up in flames and forty-three residents lost their lives. To this day, neither city has fully recovered from the "long, hot summer" of 1967.[54]

Congressman Gardner rushed to Newark to see the destruction for himself. Before leaving Washington, he read a lengthy article from *Barron's* magazine into the *Congressional Record*. It charged that the urban uprisings had been "subsidized as well as organized" by antipoverty workers and radical civil rights agitators. That message resonated back home. I. Beverly Lake Sr., who was now a justice on the North Carolina Supreme Court, congratulated Gardner on his effort. "The apostles of appeasement . . . must be removed from positions of public trust," he declared. "We must clean up the whole foul mess and fumigate the premises."[55]

Gardner's supporters agreed. "What has happened to the rights of the white people of this nation?" they asked. "People who go to work every day, pay their taxes and obey the laws of this nation. Are we the forgotten people?" And to what end would civil rights and antipoverty agitation lead? In a letter that might easily have been penned a century earlier, one woman raised the specter of black domination. "It is not inconceivable," she worried, "that those very Negroes marching will one day encircle our great Capitol building, demanding [that lawmakers] give them control of our nation, or face a 'non-violent' riot which will topple our government."[56]

In 1968, Republican presidential candidate Richard Nixon leveraged this fear and resentment to flip the upper South. His chief opponent in North Carolina was former Alabama governor George Wallace, who ran on a segregationist "law and order" platform as the American Independent Party nominee. Wallace captured 31 percent of the vote; Nixon, 40 percent. Combined, these figures revealed conservative whites' increasing willingness to stray from their grandfathers' party. Democrat Hubert H. Humphrey won only 29 percent of ballots cast in the state.[57]

Four years later, Nixon made a clean sweep of the South, and in North Carolina, other Republicans rode his coattails. Though the vast majority of white voters were still registered as Democrats, they elected James E. Holshouser Jr. governor—the first Republican to win the office since 1896—and sent Willis Smith's protégé Jesse Helms to the U.S. Senate, where he would serve for the next thirty years. This was the "uprising" that Josiah Bailey and Sim DeLapp had prophesied.

Old Wine, New Vessels

By the mid-1980s, North Carolina once again had a tightly contested two-party political system. A visitor from a similar time a century before would have been confounded by the way that party labels had flipped. Democrats now resembled the party of Lincoln, and Republicans looked like Democrats of old. But the visitor would easily have recognized the competing social visions the parties offered voters. One party stressed the importance of balancing individual rights against social responsibility, contended that government had an indispensable role to play in promoting the general welfare, and viewed the prerogatives of citizenship as the birthright of every American. The other party was wary of government infringement on personal choice and thought of equal citizenship as a privilege to be earned rather than an entitlement. In a society that for most of its history had stood on a foundation of slavery and Jim Crow, contests over these competing ideals were centered, more often than not, on the question of racial equality. Conservatives—whatever their party label—took a narrow view on that issue, partly out of racial animus but also because they understood that black enfranchisement led to progressive social policies.

This was at no time more obvious than in 1984 and 1990, when U.S. senator Jesse Helms faced two Democratic challengers: Governor James B. Hunt Jr. in the first contest, and, in the second, former Charlotte mayor Harvey B. Gantt.

After his first-term election in 1972, Helms had quickly established himself as a leading spokesman of the new Republican Party that was ascendant in North Carolina and across the nation. He did so by holding true to what I. Beverly Lake Sr. had described as the "eternal principles" of southern conservatism. Helms championed individualism and free enterprise; he opposed labor unions and attributed inequality to the values and behaviors of people who lived on society's margins; and he characterized social welfare programs as instruments of theft that rewarded the takers rather than the makers of wealth. "A lot of human beings have been born bums," Helms famously declared at the height of the civil rights movement and war on poverty. "Most of them—until fairly recently—were kept from behaving like bums because work was necessary for all who wished to eat. The more we remove penalties for being a bum, the more bumism is going to blossom."[58]

Helms had a talent for capturing the anger of white Americans who felt aggrieved by their fellow citizens' demands for rights and respect. He was also an innovative campaigner. His North Carolina Congressional Club, founded in 1978, was a fund-raising juggernaut that pioneered targeted political advertising of the sort that began with mass mailing in Helms's era and today is conducted via the internet and social media. Added to all of that, Helms was unwavering in his convictions. Supporters and adversaries alike knew him as "Senator No." He was, in the words of one sympathetic biographer, "an uncompromising ideologue."[59]

Jim Hunt, Helms's opponent in 1984, was cut from different cloth. Born in 1937, he belonged to a new generation of Democrats whose politics had been shaped by the progressive political currents of the post–World War II era. Hunt grew up on a tobacco and dairy farm in eastern North Carolina. His parents were devout New Dealers, supporters of Frank Graham, and close associates of Governor Kerr Scott. Hunt served two terms as student body president while he was an undergraduate at North Carolina State University in Raleigh, and in 1960 he managed Terry Sanford's campaign on campuses statewide.[60]

These early years taught life lessons that shaped Hunt's political career. His parents instilled a belief that government had an indispensable role to play in providing the resources that people needed to improve their lives, and from Terry Sanford he learned to appreciate the ways that Jim Crow blighted North Carolina with illiteracy, hunger, sickness, and want. During two terms as governor—from 1977 to 1985— Hunt put these lessons to work. He established a reputation as one of the South's most progressive leaders by persuading lawmakers to appropriate $281 million in new spending on public education. He also recruited high-wage industries to shift North Carolina away from its traditional cheap-labor economy, appointed former Chapel Hill mayor Howard Lee as the first black cabinet secretary in state history, and named pioneering black lawmaker Henry Frye to the North Carolina Supreme Court.[61]

As Hunt began his campaign to unseat Senator Helms in the 1984 election, he had reason to expect victory. Polls conducted in early 1983 showed him leading Helms by more than twenty percentage points. Hunt enjoyed particularly enthusiastic support among low-income whites earning less than $15,000 a year. They preferred him over Helms by a margin of 64 to 21 percent. That was a testament to the popularity of Hunt's policies on education and economic development.[62]

Events later in the year warned how quickly that lead could be undone. In early October, Helms led a four-day filibuster against legislation that eventually created a national Martin Luther King Jr. holiday. He revived a line of attack on King that he had honed during the 1960s as a nightly editorialist on Raleigh's WRAL-TV. King, he charged, was a communist revolutionary, not a peacemaker, and his actions and ideals were "not compatible with the concepts of this country." When President Reagan signed the bill into law a month later, many in the press reported a humiliating defeat for Helms. But the senator knew his audience back home. Even negative headlines helped him solidify his image as an uncompromising defender of conservative values. The effectiveness of that ploy showed in the polls. At the beginning of the race, Hunt had led Helms by thirty percentage points in counties where blacks made up less than 10 percent of the population and whites were inclined to worry more about economic opportunities than civil rights. In the months after the filibuster, that deficit turned into a ten-point lead for Helms.[63]

As one senior adviser acknowledged, the Helms campaign knew that they "couldn't beat Jim Hunt on issues," so they came out guns blazing on race. The campaign ran thousands of newspaper and radio ads that linked Hunt to the threat of a "bloc vote" being organized by black Democratic presidential candidate Jesse Jackson and other civil rights leaders. One print ad showed Hunt and Jackson sitting together in the governor's residence and warned, "Gov. James B. Hunt Jr. wants the State Board of Elections to boost minority voter registration in North Carolina. . . . Ask yourself: Is this a proper use of taxpayer funds?"[64]

As a means of courting evangelical Christian voters, the Helms campaign and its allies focused similar attacks on the emerging gay rights movement. The *Landmark*, a right-wing paper supported largely by advertising income from the Helms campaign, charged that Hunt had accepted cash contributions from "faggots, perverts, [and] sexual deviates"; that as a college student, he had a "pretty young boy" as a roommate and "lover"; and that he was, himself, "sissy, prissy, girlish, and effeminate." In a move reminiscent of the 1950 contest between Frank Graham and Willis Smith, Helms distanced himself from the specifics of those charges but reminded voters at every turn that his enemies were the "atheists, the homosexuals, the militant women's groups, the union bosses, the bloc voters, and so on." This enemies list endeared Helms to enough North Carolinians to best Hunt with 52 percent of the vote.[65]

Six years later, race was an issue by default when Harvey Gantt won the Democratic senatorial nomination. His very presence on the ticket testified to the gains that blacks had made in access to the ballot box and political influence. He was born in 1943 in the South Carolina Lowcountry, where cotton and rice barons had built their fortunes from the labor of his enslaved forebears. Gantt's parents moved the family to Charleston when Harvey was still an infant. There his father found a job in the city's navy shipyard, thanks to Roosevelt's executive order opening war industries to black workers. Gantt grew up in public housing and was educated in the city's segregated public schools. He traced his fascination with politics to his father's membership in the NAACP and to dinner table conversations about civil rights. As a high school student, Gantt joined his local NAACP Youth Council, and in April 1960, shortly after sit-in demonstrations began in North Carolina, he led similar protests in downtown Charleston.[66]

When Gantt thought about college, an obvious option was to attend a historically black institution, such as Howard University or the Tuskegee Institute. But he believed that America's future was going to be "all about" integration, so he headed off to Iowa State University, where he expected to get "an integrated education." Iowa State turned out to be as white as Howard was black. Disappointed, Gantt returned home to create the future he longed for. He tried three times to gain admission to Clemson Agricultural College (now Clemson University) but was denied. With support from the NAACP Legal Defense Fund, Gantt sued, and in 1963 he won a federal court order that he be admitted as the school's first black student. He graduated with a degree in architecture and then earned an MA in city planning from the Massachusetts Institute of Technology. Gantt made his way to Charlotte in 1971, opened an architectural firm, and quickly became involved in politics. He served on the city council from 1974 to 1983 and won election as mayor for two terms, from 1983 to 1987. When he challenged Helms in 1990, Gantt was the first black Democrat in the nation's history to run for the U.S. Senate.[67]

Helms's campaign against Gantt echoed his attacks on Hunt. When Gantt raised issues of education, health, and the environment, Helms pointed to Gantt's financial ties to "militant homosexuals." One newspaper ad asked, Why are "homosexuals buying this election?" The answer: "Because Harvey Gantt will support their demands for mandatory gay rights." At a campaign rally, Helms echoed the "White People Wake Up" warning from Willis Smith's campaign against Frank Graham. "Think about it," he said. "Homosexuals and lesbians, disgusting people marching in our streets demanding all sorts of things, including the right to marry each other. How do you like them apples?"[68]

Still, that only got Helms so far. In mid-October, some polls had him

Harvey Gantt speaks to reporters on January 28, 1963, the day of his admission to Clemson University. Courtesy of Clemson University Library, Flickr, http://bit.ly/38kFjGT.

trailing Gantt by as many as eight percentage points. It was time to play what one of Helms's advisers called "the race card." In the run-up to Election Day, the Helms campaign aired a television ad that played on white anxiety over black access to desegregated workplaces. The ad showed a white man's hands crumpling a rejection letter. He wore a wedding band and presumably had a family to support. And he was dressed in a flannel shirt, not a button-down and tie. He obviously worked with those hands. The voice-over lamented, "You needed that job and you were the best qualified. But they had to give it to a minority because of a racial quota. Is that really fair? Harvey Gantt says it is. Harvey Gantt supports . . . [a] racial quota law that makes the color of your skin more important than your qualifications. You'll vote on this issue next Tuesday. For racial quotas, Harvey Gantt. Against racial quotas, Jesse Helms." The reference to quotas arose from debate over the proposed Civil Rights Act of 1990. Conservatives charged that it included such strict antidiscrimination rules that employers would feel compelled to adopt minority hiring goals in order to preempt potential lawsuits. President George H. W. Bush vetoed the law on October

22, days before the Helms ad ran on television. There was in all of this striking irony for anyone who cared to notice it. The ad attacked the very thing that Helms and his supporters sought to protect—economic privilege based on skin color.[69]

At the same time, the state Republican Party attempted to suppress black voter turnout by mailing postcards to 125,000 voters in heavily black precincts, warning recipients incorrectly that they would not be allowed to cast a ballot if they had moved within thirty days, and that if they attempted to vote, they would be subject to prosecution and imprisonment. Helms subsequently won the election with 65 percent of the white vote and 53 percent of the vote overall. When Gantt challenged him again in 1996, the results were the same.[70]

These battles over Helms's seat in the U.S. Senate made it clear that the political realignment that had begun in the mid-1930s was all but complete. White conservatives now identified as Republicans, and a coalition of minority voters and liberal whites constituted the Democratic Party's base. Contests between the two camps were often decided by slim margins. That was evidence of how closely divided North Carolinians were in the ways that they imagined the state's future. It also revealed the profound difference that racially prejudicial appeals could make in the outcome of elections and the character of governance.

Chapter 5 Reincarnation

North Carolina politics settled into a wobbling equilibrium in the 1990s and 2000s. From 1980 until Barack Obama's election in 2008, Republicans carried North Carolina in every presidential contest. Jesse Helms remained in the Senate until his retirement in 2002 and was replaced in subsequent elections by Republican Elizabeth Dole and Democrat Kay Hagan. The state's second Senate seat swung back and forth between Republicans and Democrats in every election between 1980 and 2004. In state government, Democrats had a tighter grip on power. Republican James (Jim) G. Martin won election to the governor's office for two consecutive terms in 1984 and 1988, but after that Democrats controlled the office for twenty years. Democrats also fared well in the General Assembly, though they lost control of the lower chamber to Republicans in 1994, 1996, and 1998. The 1994 election also turned the table on the state's congressional delegation, which changed from eight Democrats and four Republicans to eight Republicans and four Democrats.[1]

While the balance of power tilted in their favor, Democrats pursued a progressive agenda that included reforms in education and health care, new protections for workers' rights and the environment, and easier access to the ballot box. But this latest era of emancipatory politics came to an abrupt end after the collapse of financial markets in 2007–8 plunged the nation into its worst economic crisis since the Great Depression. Unemployment soared to record highs as jobs were gutted in every sector of the state's economy. The anxiety that the downturn produced, together with white backlash against the election of a black president, fueled an insurgency that helped Republicans gain control of both houses of the General Assembly in 2010. On the basis of that year's federal census, lawmakers redistricted the state legislature in a way that yielded a Republican supermajority in 2012. The party's gubernatorial candidate, Pat McCrory, also won election that year. With a hold on both the legislative and executive branches of state government, Republicans began to execute a plan, years in the making, to set aside progressive policies, restrict the franchise, and restore conservative principles.

Emancipatory Politics at High Tide

Despite his loss to Jesse Helms in 1984, Jim Hunt remained popular with North Carolina voters. They knew him as a reformer and modernizer who had improved the public schools and recruited new jobs that offset the loss of employment in the state's traditional manufacturing sector—textiles, tobacco, and furniture. Hunt also had a national reputation as a leader on education policy. He worked with the Carnegie Corporation to raise teaching standards and to bring educators, scientists, and business executives together to examine the relationship between schools and economic development. In 1992, Hunt presented himself for an encore in the governor's office. He later reflected on his reasons: "I was concerned about the state and where it was headed," he said. "Education, children, infant mortality rate highest in the country, SAT scores very low, losing out on economic development to South Carolina and other states. Instead of making progress, we were going down." On the campaign trail, Hunt spoke in more optimistic terms. He told voters that he wanted "to change North Carolina," to "build a state that would be America's model." Hunt bested his Republican opponent, Lieutenant Governor Jim Gardner, by ten percentage points. In 1996, he went on to win a fourth term by an even larger margin.[2]

Over the course of eight years, Hunt and fellow Democrats in the General Assembly built on the accomplishments of his first administration. They established Smart Start, a program that pumped millions into local communities to provide affordable preschool education and improved health care to young children. In some ways, he modeled the program on Terry Sanford's North Carolina Fund. "I believed that if you built support for [early-childhood programs] at the local level," Hunt later explained, "it would be hard for anybody to take it away. Because the local people would own it. If you build it and root it at the local level, where it's their program, it's their Smart Start, it's their local partnership for the children, it would be hard to ever kill it." Hunt and lawmakers also raised teacher salaries to the national average and increased total state spending on public education from 76 to 86 percent of that average; launched Health Choice, a state program for uninsured children who were ineligible for Medicare, Medicaid, or other forms of federal assistance; and created a new Department of Juvenile Justice to address the underlying causes of youth crime. The principles that animated these initiatives were evident in Hunt's commitment to inclusive governance as well. When he left office in 2001, 22 percent of his appointees to state agencies and commissions were minorities, a figure that matched the demographics of the state.[3]

Between 1992 and 2009, Democratic lawmakers worked to sustain these achievements by expanding minority citizens' access to the franchise. Many of their reforms echoed the Fusion election law of 1895. Key legislation created an option for early voting; allowed voters who went to the wrong precinct on Election Day to cast a provisional ballot; permitted same-day registration during early voting; and created a system for preregistering sixteen- and seventeen-year-olds, so that their names would be placed on the voter rolls automatically when they turned eighteen. The net effect of these reforms was a steady increase in voter participation. In 1996, North Carolina ranked forty-third among the states for voter turnout; it rose to thirty-seventh place by 2000 and to eleventh place in 2012.[4]

Most of the increase was driven by higher rates of black political participation. Between 2000 and 2012, black voter registration surged by 51.1 percent, compared to 15.8 percent among whites. Black turnout followed apace. Between 2000 and 2008, it jumped from 41.9 to 71.5 percent. In the 2008 and 2012 elections, blacks registered and voted at higher rates than whites for the first time in North Carolina's history. That level of participation was critically important in the 2008 presidential contest, when Barack Obama won North Carolina with a slim margin of 14,171 votes out of 4,271,125 ballots cast. He was the first Democratic presidential candidate to carry the state since Jimmy Carter in 1976.[5]

Close observers of North Carolina politics noted that Hispanic[6] voters were also "indispensable" to Obama's victory. The state's Hispanic population grew more than tenfold—from just over 75,000 to more than 800,000—between 1990 and 2010. That expansion was driven by the economic boom of the 1990s and early 2000s, when immigrants poured into North Carolina to work jobs in pork and poultry processing, construction, building maintenance, and hospitality. By 2010, Hispanics represented 8.5 percent of the state's total population and 1.3 percent of registered voters. In a tight election, even that small number could change the outcome. North Carolina's Hispanic voters, most of whom favored Democrats, cast 20,468 ballots in 2008, a figure larger than Obama's winning margin.[7]

Hispanic voters' influence in state politics is likely to increase dramatically in the coming decade. Today the population stands at 997,000, roughly 10 percent of the state total, and the annual growth rate, at 24.6 percent, is a third higher than in the United States overall. Moreover, nearly 40 percent of North Carolina's current Hispanic residents are children or young teenagers who—unlike many of their parents' generation—were born in this country. Under the terms of the Fourteenth and Fifteenth Amendments, ratified during Reconstruction, they will be entitled to vote when they reach the age of eighteen. Taken together, these figures point to the potential for a new multiracial alliance of Hispanic, black, and progressive white voters.[8]

Black President, White Revolt

The 2008 presidential election cut two ways in North Carolina. It was the culmination of generations of struggle for equal citizenship and a sign of how much the state had changed since the establishment of Jim Crow a century before. To some North Carolinians, a black president in the White House seemed to mark the dawning of a new postracial era. But Obama's victory was also part of a cascade of events that led quickly to coordinated efforts to restrict voting rights and roll back decades of progressive social policy.

As historian Carol Anderson has detailed, the 2008 election was full of bad news for Republicans. At the national level, Obama attracted a larger share of the white vote than Democrat John Kerry in 2004. He also won substantial majorities among Hispanic, Asian, youth, and women voters, along with 95 percent of blacks. This loose coalition had gone to the polls to voice support for an expansive vision of government that Republicans had opposed since the days of the New Deal. They rallied to Obama's hopeful slogan, "Yes We Can," and his belief that Washington could improve people's lives with achievable reforms, such as raising the minimum wage, expanding the Earned Income Tax Credit, protecting the rights of labor, investing in public education, and guaranteeing universal access to affordable health care. Looking back on the election, Republican senator Lindsey Graham identified the problem: his party was "not generating enough angry white guys to stay in business for the long term."[9]

An economy in crisis offered the makings of a solution. When Obama took the oath of office in January 2009, a near collapse of the banking system was threatening to plunge America and the rest of the world into a second Great Depression. North Carolina was one of the states hit hardest. Within a year, the unemployment rate soared to 10.9 percent. That caused pain in every corner of the labor market, but the situation in manufacturing and construction became particularly grim. Between 2007 and 2012, those sectors experienced job losses of 18 and 32 percent, respectively. The banking crisis had begun with the implosion of the market for subprime mortgages. As more people lost their jobs, they fell behind on payments that under the best of circumstances had strained their budgets. Between 2006 and 2014, nine million American families lost their homes; in 2008 alone, the number in North Carolina was 53,995.[10]

Voters grew angry, particularly at politicians they felt had let the crisis happen and now sought to fix it with bailouts for financial institutions and corporations that were ostensibly "too big to fail." In North Carolina, that bitterness was amplified by corruption at the highest level of government. Soon after Democratic governor Michael F. Easley left office in 2009, state and federal officials opened investigations into alleged violations of campaign finance laws. Later that year, his tortured testimony before the State Board of Elections was broadcast live on television. Shortly after that spectacle, Easley entered a plea agreement on a felony charge.[11]

Voters' fury fueled the Tea Party revolt that erupted in 2009. The movement was overwhelmingly white, and its supporters' grievances echoed principles that had defined a century of conservative thought and politics. Tea Partiers rallied against big government, denounced the 2010 Affordable Care Act (Obamacare) as a socialist violation of individual liberty, criticized social welfare programs as a waste of taxpayers' money, and launched a xenophobic attack on immigrants, who they claimed were stealing American jobs, dealing in illicit drugs, and perpetrating violent crime. The Tea Party sprang from the grassroots, but soon many of its rallies were financed and orchestrated by Americans for Prosperity, a conservative political action group backed by billionaire industrialists Charles G. and David H. Koch and a national network of wealthy donors and like-minded organizations.[12]

Tea Partiers channeled much of their anger through racial invective. They hailed President Obama as "primate in chief"; they donned T-shirts that demanded, "Put the White Back in the White House"; and at rallies in Washington, D.C., they carried placards that exclaimed, "We came unarmed [this time]." In North Carolina, a member of the Charlotte-Mecklenburg Board of Education argued against increases in school spending on grounds that costs had been inflated by what he called "Obama Bucks"—a pejorative term initially applied to food stamps but soon attached to a wide variety of federal social welfare programs. Three years later, when Charlotte hosted the Democratic National Convention, V. R. Phipps, a self-styled "patriot" from eastern North Carolina, captured headlines when he parked his truck and a trailer near delegates' downtown hotels. The trailer contained effigies of the president and state political figures, each strung up lynching-style in a hangman's noose. Phipps later took his display on tour in the Midwest and up and down the East Coast.[13]

Republican leaders embraced the anger and presented themselves as the party that would defy the black president and his supporters. Shortly before the 2010 midterm elections, in which Republicans won control of the U.S. House of Representatives, Mitch McConnell, the Republican majority leader in the Senate, pledged to voters, "The single most important thing we want to achieve is for President Obama to be a one-term president. . . . You need to go out and help us finish the job." Writing a year later, Ron Unz, publisher of the *American Conservative*, an influential online political forum, described that racial logic in approving terms: "As whites become a smaller and smaller portion of the local population in more and more regions, they will naturally become ripe for political polarization based on appeals to their interests as whites. And if Republicans focus their campaigning on racially charged issues such as immigration and affirmative action, they will promote this polarization, gradually transforming the two national political parties into crude proxies for direct racial interests, effectively becoming the 'white party' and the 'non-white party.'" Unz predicted that since white voters constituted a majority of the national electorate, "the 'white party'—the Republicans—will end up controlling almost all political power and could enact whatever policies they desired, on both racial and non-racial issues."[14]

Conservative Electoral Victory, 2010

Unz's assessment read like a script for North Carolina politics in the next decade. Voter discontent offered Republicans an opportunity to extend their success in presidential and senatorial elections downward into local campaigns for seats in the state legislature. Raleigh businessman James Arthur (Art) Pope spearheaded the party's efforts to achieve that goal. Pope was chairman and CEO of Variety Wholesalers, one of the largest privately held companies in the United States. It ran more than three hundred discount stores throughout the Southeast. The family amassed a sizable fortune from that enterprise, and Pope's parents were key supporters of the North Carolina Republican Party, which acknowledged their generosity by naming its Raleigh headquarters in their honor. As a student at the University of North Carolina at Chapel Hill, Pope was a cofounder of the North Carolina Libertarian Party. He practiced law for a short time, joined the family business in 1986, and subsequently served four terms in the General Assembly as a Republican member of the state house of representatives.[15]

Like his parents, Pope invested heavily in conservative politics. He established the John Locke Foundation in 1990 and the Civitas Institute in 2005. Both are located in Raleigh. They are state equivalents of the Heritage Foundation and the American Enterprise and Cato Institutes. Like those organizations, the Locke Foundation and Civitas engage in policy research and advocacy around issues such as taxation, public education, and social welfare. Civitas, in particular, has defined its goal as charting a new course for a state it claims is "dominated by leftist policies and politicians."[16]

After 2008, the Pope-funded think tanks made election law reform a priority. They produced a steady stream of articles, op-eds, and blog posts on voter fraud and the need for a strict photo ID law, an end to same-day registration, and shorter early-voting periods. The Locke Foundation was particularly keen to connect the threat of voter fraud to immigration and the presence of what it called a "large illegal alien population." In a 2010 report, the Foundation suggested that immigrants could easily take advantage of same-day registration by "flooding" polling places at the last minute and casting ballots before election officials had time to check their IDs and Social Security numbers. The report also warned that staff from the Mexican consulate in Raleigh were "traveling throughout the state monthly to provide Consular IDs to Mexican nationals," who could then use the documents to "obtain driver's licenses, apply for food stamps and other public benefits, or even register to vote." The Locke Foundation knew the latter part of that claim to be false but repeated it nonetheless. In the Republican lexicon, "voter fraud" took on the meaning that conservative Democrats had once attributed to "bloc voting."[17]

In the mid-2000s, Art Pope worked behind the scenes to pressure moderate Republicans to be more partisan. He did so by funding, and threatening to fund, challengers in primary elections. After having some success in moving the Republican Party to the right, he turned his attention to unseating Democrats. In 2010, judgments in two federal lawsuits facilitated that effort. The U.S. Supreme Court ruled in *Citizens United v. Federal Election Commission* that under the First Amendment's protection of free speech, corporations, nonprofit organizations, and similar entities were entitled to spend unlimited sums on political communications, so long as they did not contribute directly to a candidate's campaign. This removed the restrictions that had been imposed by federal law. A subsequent judgment by the U.S. Court of Appeals for the District of Columbia in *Speechnow.org v. Federal Election Commission* extended that protection to individuals who contributed to organizations like those specified in *Citizens United*.[18]

In 2010, Pope and other conservative strategists targeted twenty-two Democrats in the General Assembly who were up for reelection. They backed Republican challengers with $2.2 million contributed by Pope and members of his family, along with Variety Wholesalers. The money was channeled through the state Republican Party and three nonprofit organizations: Civitas Action and Real Jobs N.C., both established and financed primarily by Pope, and Americans for Prosperity, the national political advocacy organization directed by the Koch brothers, with whom Pope had a long and close relationship.[19]

Racial appeals figured prominently in the 2010 campaign. Take, for example, the effort to unseat John J. Snow Jr., a state senator from western North Carolina, and L. Hugh Holliman, Democratic majority leader in the state house of representatives. Both had voted for the 2009 Racial Justice Act, which gave inmates the right to challenge imposition of the death penalty by using statistical evidence to prove that race was a factor in their sentencing. A mass mailing from the executive committee of the state Republican Party attacked the law and its backers. The oversized postcard featured a photograph of Henry L. McCollum, who had been convicted of raping and killing an eleven-year-old girl. It warned that "thanks to ultra-liberal [lawmakers]" like Holliman and Snow, McCollum "might be moving out of jail and into Your *neighborhood* sometime soon." The not-so-subtle message was that recipients who cared for their families' safety would vote to "get rid of criminal coddler[s]" and keep men like McCollum "where they belong."[20]

There was a double layer of tragedy in this racial appeal. Holliman, a staunch defender of the death penalty, had lost a sixteen-year-old

The North Carolina Republican Executive Committee used this flier and a similar mailing to target Democrats Hugh Holliman and John Snow for their support of the 2009 Racial Justice Act. Courtesy of *WRAL.com*.

daughter to murder decades earlier. He and many of the public found the postcard so offensive that they demanded an apology from Tom Fetzer, state chairman of the Republican Party. Fetzer obliged but also took the opportunity to criticize Holliman's vote for the racial justice law. Then, in 2014, McCollum was exonerated and released from prison. The *New York Times* reported that the case against him, "always weak, fell apart after DNA evidence implicated another man" who "lived only a block from where the victim's body was found" and "had admitted to committing a similar rape and murder around the same time."[21]

Conservative activists disparaged North Carolina's growing Hispanic population in comparable ways. In 2009, Jeff Mixon, legislative director in the Raleigh office of Americans for Prosperity, attacked Hispanic immigrants as deadbeats and thugs. He described North Carolina as a "magnet for illegals" who came to America to "take advantage [of a] vast array of benefits . . . from food stamps and free medical care to in-state tuition at our community colleges." He also played on historically familiar prejudices that associate dark skin with criminality. "Poor illegal aliens" deserved no sympathy, he argued, because they provided cover for "wolves among the sheep"—members of Mexican "narco gangs" who threatened to "ruin our communities."[22]

In the 2010 campaign, the executive committee of the North Carolina Republican Party played on such anti-immigrant sentiments in a mailer

The North Carolina Republican Executive Committee produced this flier to insinuate that Democrat Chris Heagarty's stance on tax issues was somehow connected to the interests of Hispanic immigrants. Courtesy of *IndyWeek*.

it distributed to support candidate Thomas O. Murry, who was running against sitting Democrat John Christopher Heagarty for the District 41 house seat in the General Assembly. With a sombrero atop his head and his skin darkened by clever photo editing, "Señor" Heagarty exclaims, "Mucho taxo"—a reference to policies that Republicans charged were driving away jobs.[23]

On Election Day, Snow, Holliman, Heagarty, and fifteen of the other Democrats on Art Pope's hit list lost their seats, giving Republicans a majority in both houses of the state legislature. Republican lawmakers subsequently consolidated their hold on power. In 2011, they gerrymandered legislative districts to favor their interests, and the following year they won a supermajority in the General Assembly. That effort was part of REDMAP (short for Redistricting Majority Party), a national strategy for increasing Republican strength in both the U.S. Congress and state legislatures. Voters in the 2012 election also sent Republican Patrick L. (Pat) McCrory to the governor's office. He defeated Democrat Walter H. Dalton, the sitting lieutenant governor, who had entered the race late and with limited funds when Governor Bev Purdue announced that she would not seek reelection.[24]

Seven months later, the U.S. Supreme Court gave North Carolina Republicans a gift. In *Shelby County v. Holder*, the court struck down section 5 of the Voting Rights Act, which safeguarded the rights of protected minorities by requiring federal preclearance of changes in voting procedures. The enormity of that decision cannot be overstated. It opened the way to dismantling hard-won protections that had been vital to dismantling Jim Crow discrimination and reenfranchising minority citizens.

House Bill 589

Within hours of the *Shelby* ruling, Republican leaders announced that they planned to introduce a bill that would modify the ways North Carolinians registered to vote and cast their ballots. Lawmakers had, in fact, been working on draft legislation for some time. As early as January 2012, a member of the legislative staff had asked the State Board of Elections, "Is there any way to get a breakdown of the 2008 voter turnout, by race (white and black) and type of vote (early and Election Day)?" A year later, a Republican lawmaker wondered, "Is there no category for 'Hispanic' voter?" Another asked officials at the University of North Carolina "about the number of Student ID cards that are created and the percentage of those who are African American," and in April 2013, an aide for the Speaker of the House requested "a breakdown, by race, of those registered voters [who] do not have a driver's license number." What eventually emerged was HB 589, legislation that targeted the strengthening multiracial coalition in the Democratic Party.[25]

Like the Act to Regulate Elections that opponents of Fusion crafted in 1899, HB 589 made no explicit reference to race or ethnicity. Nevertheless, it threatened to limit political participation by nonwhite minorities. The law included a number of provisions that would have made voting harder for black and Hispanic electors.

HB 589 required that in-person voters provide one of eight approved forms of photo identification in order to cast a ballot. Blacks constituted 22 percent of registered voters in North Carolina, but according to an analysis of State Board of Elections data by political science and election scholars Michael Herron and Daniel Smith, they represented a third of the registered voters who at the time did not possess the two most common forms of identification: a valid driver's license or a state-issued nonoperators ID card.[26]

The law also eliminated the first week of early voting, same-day registration, and straight-ticket voting. Statistics from the 2008 election in North Carolina suggested that these changes would have a disproportionately negative effect on black voter participation. In the run-up to Election Day, 71 percent of black voters cast their ballots early, including 23 percent who did so within the first week of the early voting period. That compared, respectively, to 51 and 14 percent of whites. Thirty-five percent of same-day voter registrants were black, a figure more than 50 percent higher than what might have been predicted on the basis of population statistics, and Democrats voted a straight ticket by a two-to-one ratio over Republicans.[27]

HB 589 targeted young future voters in similar fashion. It ended a program that permitted sixteen- and seventeen-year-olds to preregister at their high schools and other public sites. That opportunity had been particularly popular among black teenagers. Blacks constituted 27 percent of the pool of preregistered youth, once again a figure that was significantly higher than black representation in the general population.[28]

Many observers at the time noted this disproportionate effect on black electors, but most missed something equally important. The elimination of preregistration for sixteen- and seventeen-year-olds was remarkably forward looking: it stood to diminish the political impact of rapid growth in the number of Hispanic voters — growth that observers identified as the "future of progressive strength in America." A report from the University of North Carolina's Population Center explained the details. In 2012, as illustrated in the graph opposite, most of the state's adult Hispanic residents were noncitizens, and only 41 percent were eligible to vote, but just over the horizon, Republicans faced a large population of young Hispanics who had been born in the United States, would soon cast a ballot, and, polling data showed, were inclined to support Democrats. Demographers estimated that 72 percent of Hispanics who turned eighteen between 2012 and 2015 would be citizens. That figure rose to 84 percent of those who would turn eighteen between 2015 and 2020, and to 98 percent of those who would do so between 2020 and 2030. For Republicans, there was little to be gained and much to be risked by preregistering these future voters.[29]

Finally, HB 589 changed the rules for challenging voters' eligibility to cast a ballot and, by doing so, heightened the potential for intimidation. Three revisions were important in this regard. First, residents throughout the state were now allowed to inspect and challenge registration records in any of North Carolina's one hundred counties. In the past, challengers were permitted to act only in the counties in which they re-

North Carolina Hispanic Population by Age & Citizenship, 2012

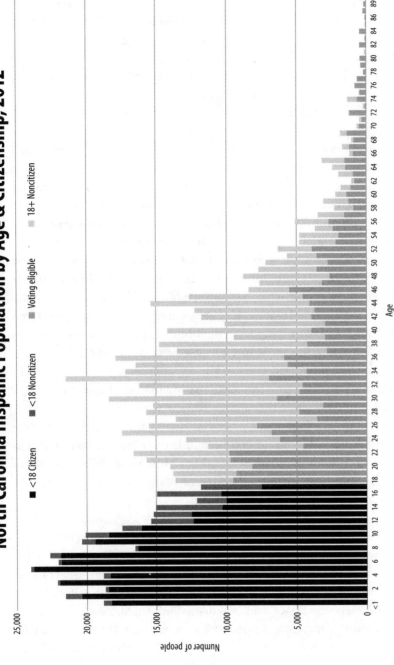

The darkest bars represent the number of Hispanic citizens who were eligible to vote in 2012 and the number of those who were then under the age of eighteen but would become eligible in the near future.

Courtesy of Carolina Demography, Carolina Population Center, University of North Carolina at Chapel Hill.

sided. Second, residents of a county were permitted to challenge voters' eligibility to cast a ballot at polling sites countywide, not just in the precincts where they themselves were registered. Third, party chairs in each county were permitted to appoint ten at-large observers to monitor voting at any polling place they believed warranted close supervision. These poll watchers would be appointed in addition to the election judges assigned to specific voting sites.

Worry that these provisions would encourage frivolous challenges and voter intimidation was based on more than speculation. During the 2012 election, a loose confederation of conservative activists mobilized by True the Vote, state-level Voter Integrity Projects, and the Madison Project launched a campaign they called Code Red USA. Their aim was to marshal a "cavalry" of volunteer poll watchers to police alleged voter fraud in battleground states, including North Carolina. In one incident, self-appointed watchdogs in Wake County petitioned to have more than five hundred voters, most of them people of color, removed from the registration rolls. Though the attempt failed, it echoed a similar episode during Reconstruction, when a group of whites in the same county challenged 150 newly freed black voters on grounds that they had registered fraudulently. As a researcher from the Brennan Center for Justice at the New York University School of Law observed, the 1872 challenge was "one of the first organized attempts by private citizens . . . to systematically undermine black political participation in North Carolina—a practice that would continue throughout the Jim Crow era."[30]

When pressed on the many ways that HB 589 threatened to limit free and fair access to the ballot box, Republican lawmakers insisted that their intent was not to infringe on voting rights. Thom Tillis, Speaker of the House, encouraged the public to think of the law instead as a means of "restoring confidence in government."[31]

Retrenchment

HB 589 was not crafted in a vacuum. As the Civitas Institute explained, it was part of a larger legislative agenda aimed at "unraveling generations of . . . liberal policies." In the 2013–14 legislative session, the Republican supermajority rolled back criminal justice reform and cut or restricted investments in education, health, and social welfare. This was what conservatives meant by their campaign pledge to "take back America." Had Furnifold Simmons, Charles Aycock, and Josephus Daniels still been alive, they would have applauded that rallying cry. It echoed their efforts more than a century before to "redeem" North Carolina from principles of equal citizenship and democratic governance.[32]

One of Republicans' top priorities was to repeal the Racial Justice Act, which Democrats had put on the books after decades of effort to abolish or reform the death penalty. Democratic leaders defended the law by pointing to a simple set of numbers: between 1977 and 2010, North Carolina courts had sent 392 people to death row, 49 percent of whom were black—a figure more than double blacks' representation in the general population. Opponents were not impressed. Thomas Goolsby, a Republican state senator and sponsor of repeal legislation, insisted that the Racial Justice Act was unnecessary because inmates on death row already had "multiple avenues of appeal." Governor Pat McCrory seconded that claim, arguing that the law did nothing more than create a new "judicial loophole to avoid the death penalty and not a path to justice." Timothy K. (Tim) Moore, who later became the state's Speaker of the House, heaped ridicule atop McCrory's scorn. "The Racial Justice Act tries to put a carte blanche solution on the problem," he said. "A white supremacist who murdered an African American could argue he was a victim of racism if blacks were on the jury." There was, of course, no evidence of black persecution of white supremacists, or that county prosecutors were eager to empanel black jurors. In fact, district attorneys in North Carolina struck eligible black jurors at roughly 2.5 times the rate they excluded all others. In early June 2013, lawmakers voted largely along party lines to rescind the Racial Justice Act, and Governor McCrory quickly signed the repeal into law.[33]

In a series of other related actions, Republican lawmakers made life more difficult for some of North Carolina's most vulnerable citizens. Nearly one million households were affected when the General Assembly abolished the state's Earned Income Tax Credit (EITC). That state program (not to be confused with the federal EITC) had been introduced in 2007 to reduce the tax liability of low- to moderate-income families, and, in many cases, provide them a refund. Economists across the political spectrum generally agree that the EITC is one of the most effective means not only of lifting people out of poverty but also of preventing them from becoming poor in the first place. Studies show that most beneficiaries claimed the credit for only one or two years; in those cases, the EITC helped families survive short-term crises, such as the loss of a job or a major medical expense. Republican lawmakers explained their decision to end the benefit by arguing that it cost too much (though the largest credit any family could claim was $294); that there was "lots of fraud in it"; and that it killed jobs by burdening small businesses with unnecessary taxes.[34]

Republicans further undercut struggling households by making deep cuts to unemployment compensation, even though North Carolina had the fifth-highest jobless rate in the nation. In 2009, the state, like most others, began to borrow funds from the federal government to cover the cost of a steep uptick in unemployment claims. By 2013, North Carolina owed more than $2 billion. To pay down that debt, Republicans in the General Assembly overhauled the state's unemployment insurance program. They imposed a temporary surtax on employers and then changed the rules for claimants who were out of work. Under the new plan, the maximum weekly benefit was reduced from $535 to $350, and the maximum duration of benefits fell from twenty-six weeks to as few as twelve. Republican lawmakers also made significant changes to the rules governing eligibility. In the past, workers could claim benefits if their hours dropped by 20 percent; under the new rules, that threshold rose to 50 percent. Workers also lost their eligibility if they were offered a job that paid 120 percent of their weekly benefit. That forced many jobseekers into low-wage, part-time employment. Five years after these reforms, though North Carolina had a $3.17 billion surplus in its coffers, the state's unemployment insurance program was the stingiest in the nation. It covered the smallest proportion of unemployed workers (10 percent) and paid the lowest average weekly benefit ($247) for the second-shortest period of eligibility. These figures represented a remarkable decline for a state that had once ranked "in the middle of the pack." Republican state representative Dana Bumgardner said of the situation, "I think where we are [now] is a good thing."[35]

The Republican majority in the General Assembly landed another blow when it refused federal funds—available under the Affordable Care Act—to extend Medicaid coverage to more than 460,000 low-income North Carolinians. That decision had a terrible cost. A study commissioned by Greensboro's Cone Health Foundation and the Winston-Salem-based Kate B. Reynolds Charitable Trust concluded that by 2016 North Carolina had forfeited $6.02 billion in federal Medicaid payments and as many as thirty thousand new jobs in health care and auxiliary services. Another report from researchers at the Harvard School of Medicine concluded that had North Carolina expanded Medicaid coverage, there would have been in the first year:

- 45,571 fewer cases of undiagnosed depression,
- 27,044 more diabetics receiving life-saving medication,
- 12,051 more women receiving mammograms, and 27,840 more being screened for cervical cancer, and
- 14,766 fewer individuals burdened by catastrophic medical expenses.

Most significant, the study estimated that 455 to 1,145 fewer of North Carolina's poorest citizens would have died.[36]

Even though the federal government would have borne the full cost of expansion in the first three years, and 90 percent after that, Speaker of the House Tim Moore argued that granting more North Carolinians access to health care was "not the right decision." "We're grappling with trying to control Medicaid spending we already have," he explained. "Creating more expense doesn't seem the prudent course." Republican senator Ralph Hise suggested that budget was not the only consideration. He and other lawmakers also worried that the beneficiaries of Medicaid expansion might get more help than they deserved. "I don't think there's any interest at the General Assembly in moving forward," he said, unless the federal government agreed to lower the income cutoff for Medicaid coverage and raise patients' copayments for care. Few members of the majority party expressed similar concern for the human cost of untreated sickness and early death, or acknowledged the economic inefficiency of a system that denies assistance to thousands of people until they are desperately ill and the cost of treatment breaks the budgets of families and hospitals alike.[37]

North Carolina's schoolchildren and teachers also ran afoul of Republican lawmakers, who mounted a stepwise campaign to weaken public education and expand private alternatives. In the process, they shortchanged a growing number of at-risk students.

The starting point was an issue that had been front and center in the 2012 campaign: a projected $3 billion shortfall in the state budget. There were obvious ways to address that problem. Lawmakers could raise taxes, cut spending, or do some of both. The Republican majority in the General Assembly chose austerity, and because expenditures on education accounted for nearly 40 percent of North Carolina's annual budget, public schools were in the bullseye. For fiscal year 2014, the total appropriation for K–12 education, when adjusted for inflation, fell $563 million short of school spending in fiscal year 2008. Included in that figure were deep cuts in funding for pre-K programs, teaching positions, transportation, textbooks, and construction.[38]

Teachers were hit particularly hard by the budget reductions and related policy changes. Early in the 2013 legislative session, Republican lawmakers sought to limit the North Carolina Association of Educators' ability to lobby by abolishing payroll deductions for teachers' membership dues. That maneuver failed when a state court ruled that it was "retaliatory" and violated teachers' right to free speech. Other attacks on teachers were more successful. The General Assembly lifted the cap on classroom size, cut funding for teaching assistants, abolished tenure, eliminated bonuses for teachers with graduate degrees, and shut down the North Carolina Teaching Fellows program, a highly effective initiative that addressed the state's chronic teacher shortage by providing scholarships to undergraduate students who planned to pursue careers in the classroom. Republican lawmakers also played a smoke-and-mirrors game with teacher salaries. After the financial crisis of 2007–8, five consecutive years without a pay raise caused teacher compensation in North Carolina to fall from twenty-second to forty-seventh place in the nation. When lawmakers made a new $282 million investment in teacher salaries in 2013, state senator Philip E. (Phil) Berger boasted that it would be "the largest teacher pay raise in state history." In total, perhaps, but the average teacher received a yearly increase of only $270. That left North Carolina dead last in the percentage change in teacher pay between 2003–4 and 2013–14. Soon teachers were fleeing the state's public schools; some dropped out of the profession, and others were lured away by better compensation in neighboring states.[39]

Budget cuts and teacher attrition created a public perception of crisis, which was amplified by changes in the way that state officials reported school performance. In 2012, the General Assembly created a simplified system that distilled a variety of measurements into letter grades that ranged from A to F. A year later, 707 public schools received a "failing" grade of D or F. Parents and educators were shocked, in part because officials failed to tell them that nearly all of the underperforming schools were also high-poverty schools, where children needed more, not less, funding for supplemental instruction, pre-K and after-school programs, lower student-teacher ratios, and reduced class size.[40]

Republican lawmakers ignored those needs and instead used the low grades to argue for increased public support for charter schools and implementation of a new freedom-of-choice voucher program for private and religious academies. These policy decisions are likely to accelerate school resegregation, which has been gathering speed since 1999, when a federal district court overturned a decades-old decision in *Swann v. Charlotte-Mecklenburg Board of Education*. The *Swann* ruling, issued in 1971, had made busing a preferred means of desegregation and, in Charlotte, led to the creation of one of the nation's most integrated school systems. But behind that success lay deep racial anxiety, which led a group of white parents to initiate the court challenge to *Swann* in 1997 and, more broadly, informed the creation of North Carolina's charter school program that same year. A Duke University study of charter schools in the period between 1998 and 2012 offered insight into these developments and their role in resegregation. The Duke researchers found that white parents preferred schools that were no more than 20 percent black. Beyond that tipping point, they began to look for alternatives. The results showed in the demography of North Carolina schools. In 2012, only about 30 percent of students in the traditional public education system attended highly segregated schools that were more than 80 percent or less than 20 percent black. In charter schools, the figures were reversed; more than two-thirds of students were enrolled in schools that were overwhelmingly white or black. The Duke team concluded from these numbers that "North Carolina's charter schools have become a way for white parents to secede from the public school system, as they once did to escape racial integration orders."[41]

North Carolina's voucher program also works to undermine confidence in public schools and encourage resegregation. The program uses public school funds to offer Opportunity Scholarships to low-income families that earn less than 133 percent of the federal poverty line. The State Department of Public Instruction markets the vouchers, valued at up to $4,200 a year, as assistance for parents who wish to remove their students from high-poverty, underresourced schools—that is, underperforming schools created by state policies. Today, 93 percent of voucher recipients attend religious schools, which, on average, do not serve them particularly well. North Carolina accountability standards for voucher-eligible schools are among the most lenient in the nation. Those schools are not required to seek accreditation, employ licensed teachers, comply with state curriculum standards, or administer end-of-year evaluations of student learning. Given that lax oversight, it is not surprising that in the small number of voucher-eligible schools that do report results from standardized reading and math tests, 54 percent of students score below national averages. Enrollment data for voucher-eligible schools is not readily available, but information from disparate sources suggests that they are an increasingly attractive choice for white families who are looking for an alternative to integrated public schools. Between the 2014–15 and 2016–17 academic years, the share of vouchers claimed by black students fell from 49 to 35 percent, while the share used by whites increased from 27 to 41 percent. One fact provides at least a partial explanation of that shift: in large religious schools with more than eighty voucher students, average enrollment was 89 percent white.[42]

Restoring "blindfolded" justice that dismissed four centuries of racial brutality in American jurisprudence; abandoning the poor, the sick, and the unemployed; and defaulting on North Carolina's constitutional obligation to provide all children "equal opportunities" in school—this was the agenda that Republicans enacted after their sweep of the General Assembly and governor's office in 2012. On election night in 2016, as he celebrated Donald J. Trump's presidential victory, Tim Moore, the state Speaker of the House, looked back on his party's handiwork and exclaimed, "We've had a great four years since we took the majority." But even in that moment of triumph, Moore and other party leaders knew that candidates with different priorities might prevail in future elections and sweep away Republicans' accomplishments.[43]

How, then, to make the conservative revolution permanent? One answer—the answer that Charles Aycock and white-rule Democrats had imposed in 1900—was to disenfranchise dissenting voters. That was the purpose of HB 589, which a federal court would later describe as "the most restrictive voting law North Carolina has seen since the era of Jim Crow." Another answer was to create a chronic budget "crisis" by placing a cap on taxation, so that the reply to any demand citizens might make on their government would be, "We can't afford it." That is what Republicans did between 2013 and 2019, when they replaced North Carolina's progressive income tax with a 5.25 percent flat tax, cut corporate tax rates from 6.9 to 2.5 percent, and expanded the list of goods and services that were subject to a regressive sales tax. These changes shifted the tax burden downward onto North Carolina's least affluent citizens. The poorest quintile, who earned an average income of $11,400, paid 9.5 percent in state and local taxes; the middle quintile, who had an average income of $40,100, paid 9.4 percent; and those at the very top—the richest 1 percent—paid 6.4 percent of their earnings. In 2018, Republican lawmakers cemented this redistribution into the state constitution. They proposed, and a majority of voters ratified, an amendment that limited the state income tax to 7 percent—an inviolable cap, regardless of North Carolinians' needs. North Carolina was only the second state to impose such a restriction. Georgia was the other.[44]

Republicans in the General Assembly had the votes to brush aside Democrats' objections to their overhaul of public policy, but public outrage would not be so easily dismissed. Indeed, it invaded the halls of the legislature. Over the course of thirteen consecutive weeks during the summer of 2013, great crowds of protestors gathered in public spaces around the legislative building in Raleigh, and nearly a thousand were arrested for singing freedom songs in the lobbies outside the chambers of the state senate and house. In the second week, protestors named their cause the Moral Monday movement. Led by Reverend William Barber, a Goldsboro minister and president of the state conference of the NAACP, Moral Mondays attracted a racial and ethnic rainbow of participants. They came from every trade and profession; they were old and young, gay and straight; they were Jews, Christians, Muslims, and nonbelievers who stood side by side to demand what Reverend Barber called "a third Reconstruction." Moral Monday marches spread across North Carolina in 2014, and to cities around the nation during that year and those that followed. The largest protest took place in Raleigh in February 2017, when more than eighty thousand people filled the streets, motivated in part by a year-long controversy over the Republican legislature's passage of House Bill 2, a peculiar law that targeted both transgender people and low-wage workers. The law denied the former group protection from discrimination and prohibited cities and counties from aiding the latter by setting local minimum wage standards.[45]

Governor Pat McCrory and other Republican leaders wrote off Moral Monday protests as the work of "outsiders"—an old segregationists' complaint from the civil rights era—and the conservative Civitas Institute mocked the movement as a "circus." Even so, Civitas found the demonstrations unsettling enough to warrant the creation of a public database that identified arrested protestors by name, home address, and place of employment. That tactic reminded many observers of the white Citizens' Councils of the 1950s and 1960s, which had published "in local newspapers the names of NAACP supporters and those who signed antisegregation petitions in order to encourage retaliation against them." Such bullying stood in contrast to the principles that found expression

Teachers joined the Moral Monday marches in 2013 to protest cuts in state spending on public education. Courtesy of twbuckner, Flickr, http://bit.ly/2OMYCRH.

at the weekly protests outside the legislature. Moral Monday was a new Fusion movement, animated by commitments—religious and secular—to human equality, democratic governance, and the duty of citizens to care for one another. These convictions steered people of conscience into the streets, into jail, and, ultimately, into court.[46]

House Bill 589 in Court

In 2013, the North Carolina State Conference of the NAACP, the League of Women Voters, and the U.S. Department of Justice challenged HB 589 in the U.S. District Court for the Middle District of North Carolina. The lead plaintiff in the NAACP lawsuit was Rosanell Eaton, who had grown up in eastern North Carolina and was ninety-two years old at the time of the filing. Eaton was the granddaughter of slaves, a retired public school teacher, and a civil rights activist who had first registered to vote in 1942. In order to pass the literacy test, she memorized the preamble to the U.S. Constitution. In court, lawyers argued that HB 589 would restrict her ability to vote early, which she had done for a number of years, and to "assist others to vote, including the elderly and disabled in her community," who had come to rely on her for advice and transportation. Eaton was also likely to encounter trouble with the new photo ID requirement, because the name on her birth certificate did not match her driver's license or her voter registration card. On these grounds, the NAACP lawyers asserted that HB 589 constituted an "outright denial or dilution" of the right to vote, "or, at the very least, [imposed] substantial and undue burdens" on that right which were "not outweighed by a legitimate or compelling state interest."[47]

Presiding Judge Thomas D. Schroeder was not persuaded. He noted that "North Carolina had recently become progressive nationally by permitting absentee voting; in-person voting for up to seventeen days in addition to Election Day; additional registration after the cut-off, including up to three days before Election Day; the casting of a ballot on Election Day in any unassigned precinct in the voter's county; and 'pre-registration' by sixteen-year-olds." Democrats made these changes to improve their electoral advantage, Schroeder reasoned, and when Republicans rolled them back, they merely "retrenched" to the status quo ante. In other words, the issue at stake in HB 589 was partisanship, not voting rights. Schroeder concluded that under the new law, minorities would continue to "enjoy equal and constitutionally-compliant opportunity to participate in the electoral process."[48]

In July 2016, the U.S. Court of Appeals for the Fourth Circuit reversed Schroeder's decision on grounds that he had "fundamentally erred" in his evaluation of the case. A three-judge panel found compelling evidence of discriminatory intent in HB 589. They pointed to "the inextricable link between race and politics in North Carolina," Republican lawmakers' interest in race-specific data on voting practices, and—most important of all—the bill's timing. In addition to following closely on the heels of the *Shelby County* decision, HB 589 was also situated at a critical juncture in North Carolina politics. The appellate court judges noted that "after years of preclearance and expansion of voting access . . . African Americans were poised to act as a major electoral force." Republican lawmakers "took away that opportunity because [blacks] were about to exercise it," and they did so, the judges added, "with almost surgical precision." The Fourth Circuit panel concluded that, "because of race," North Carolina lawmakers enacted "one of the largest restrictions of the franchise" in the state's history. They remanded the HB 589 case to the district court, with instructions to enjoin the voter ID requirement and changes made to early voting, same-day registration, out-of-precinct voting, and teen preregistration.[49]

Because of race? The court was only half right. HB 589 surely bore the mark of racial animus, but Republican lawmakers did not seek to disenfranchise black and Hispanic voters simply because of their skin color. They understood that those voters are—now, as in the past—crucial to the formation of progressive alliances that cut across racial, ethnic, and class divisions and promote an expansive vision of what democracy looks like. Citizens who are drawn to these fusion movements view government not as the enemy of the people but as a means to advance human flourishing and to enlarge access to the resources that give freedom substance and meaning in everyday life—a good job, a good education, good health, and a good home. For conservatives, the problem on Election Day is not that these people will commit voter fraud but that they will use the ballot box and the machinery of government to make claims against the private hoarding of wealth and privilege. Caricatures of indolent and menacing blacks conveyed that animus in the post-Emancipation era, and it has reemerged in our time in stories of welfare queens, wasteful Obamabucks, and immigrants who steal jobs and mooch off public benefits.

Republican leaders quickly regrouped after the Fourth Circuit ruling. They began to prepare an appeal to the Supreme Court and, in the interim, attempted to salvage some of the advantage that HB 589 would have given them in the upcoming 2016 general election. In mid-August, Republican governor Pat McCrory petitioned Chief Justice John G. Roberts Jr. to reinstate the law's photo ID requirement, which had been implemented months earlier in the spring primaries. Roberts declined. At the same time, Dallas Woodhouse, executive director of the state Republican Party, encouraged county election boards to press ahead with what he called "party line changes" to early voting. The boards no longer had legal authority to shorten the early-voting period, but they could achieve much the same effect by reducing the number of early-voting sites and cutting the hours they would be open.[50]

Seventeen county boards, mostly in the east, did just that. Had section 5 of the Voting Rights Act still been in force, the changes would have required preclearance from the Department of Justice, but that was no longer a hurdle. In the affected counties, the number of ballots cast by black electors declined significantly through much of the early voting period and caught up to 2012 levels only after a herculean get-out-the-vote effort organized by the Democratic Party and like-minded advocacy organizations. Tellingly, Republican Party officials reported the initial decline in black voter participation in explicitly racial terms. The "North Carolina Obama coalition" was "crumbling," they announced in a public statement. "As a share of Early Voters, African Americans are down 6.0% . . . and Caucasians are up 4.2%."[51]

In January 2017, the U.S. Supreme Court declined to review the Fourth Circuit ruling on HB 589. Chief Justice Roberts did not offer a reason, except to reference the "blizzard of filings over who is and who is not authorized to seek review in this Court under North Carolina law." By the time the court considered the state's petition for a writ of certiorari, the newly elected governor, Roy A. Cooper III, and attorney general, Joshua Stein, both Democrats, had announced that they would drop the appeal. Republican leaders in the General Assembly tried to intervene as appellants, but that effort raised questions about their authority to do so under the state constitution. The Fourth Circuit ruling stood, though Chief Justice Roberts cautioned that the Supreme Court's refusal to consider the case on procedural grounds should not be construed as an "expression of opinion" on its merits.[52]

Constitutional Amendment, A New-Old Strategy

Following this defeat, state Republican leaders—including party chairman Robin Hayes, Senate President Pro Tempore Phil Berger, and Speaker of the House Tim Moore—vowed that they would "continue to fight." Having failed to secure a comprehensive revision of election law, they narrowed their focus to voter ID and shifted the battle to the state constitution, where similar struggles over voting rights, race, and democracy had been waged in 1868 and again in 1900. In 2018, they drafted an amendment that would require photographic identification of all electors "offering to vote in person," and they placed it on the ballot for ratification in the upcoming November election. That was a shrewd tactical move. If the amendment won voters' approval, its architect would be able to present a restriction on the franchise as the will of the people rather than a play for partisan advantage.[53]

Over the course of the campaign, Republicans argued for the amendment as a reasonable, necessary, and common-sense reform. It was reasonable, they said, because the state had made adequate provision for its citizens to acquire a photo ID, with the effect that failure to present

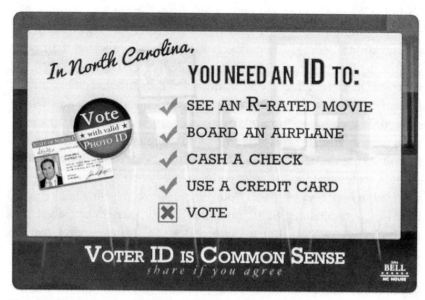

In North Carolina, **YOU NEED AN ID TO:**

✓ SEE AN R-RATED MOVIE

✓ BOARD AN AIRPLANE

✓ CASH A CHECK

✓ USE A CREDIT CARD

✗ VOTE

VOTER ID IS COMMON SENSE
share if you agree

Voter ID campaign card, Republican John Bell, N.C. House of Representatives, Twitter, October 29, 2018, http://bit.ly/2HiGE56.

the credential would be neutral on matters of race and ethnicity, wealth and poverty. The amendment was necessary, proponents claimed, because widespread voter fraud, particularly among immigrant and minority populations, threatened the integrity of elections. And requiring a photo ID to vote made sense because similar proof of identity was required to "board an airplane, see an R-rated movie, cash a check, or use a credit card."[54]

None of these justifications stood up to close scrutiny. While blacks make up 23 percent of registered voters in North Carolina, they account for 34 percent of those who have no photo ID. Why? Because they are more likely than whites not to own a car and to live in rural areas where driver license agencies are widely scattered and public transportation is limited or nonexistent. As for fraud, there is no evidence of significant dishonesty at the ballot box. In a 2016 audit, the State Board of Elections found that questionable ballots accounted for just over 0.01 percent of the 4,769,640 total votes cast. Of the 508 cases of possible fraud that the board identified, only one involved the kind of in-person deception that a photo ID requirement might have prevented. In that instance, a voter impersonated her recently deceased mother, whom she described to election officials as "a tremendous Donald Trump fan." The notion of common sense fares no better. Theaters have no legal obligation to check moviegoers' photo IDs; the Transportation Safety Administration routinely allows passengers to board planes without a photo ID, so long as they can present other forms of identification; the American Express merchant guide imposes no photo ID requirement on authorized credit card customers; and Visa and Mastercard require a photo ID only for face-to-face cash disbursements, not purchases.[55]

These points of fact notwithstanding, voters approved the constitutional amendment in November 2018 by a margin of 55.49 to 44.51 percent. Conservatives carried the day, in part because they had effectively undermined faith in the electoral process by convincing voters that fraud was widespread but remained invisible because there were no laws to expose it. Dallas Woodhouse put it this way: "Millions of North Carolinians *believe* that there is voter fraud. Now, somebody can disagree with them, but they believe it. So, adding confidence into the system is a very important thing."[56]

Republican lawmakers entered 2019 in a triumphal mood, but potentially crippling setbacks lay ahead. In September, a three-judge Superior Court panel in Wake County threw out the gerrymandered legislative districts that Republicans had first created in 2011 as part of their strategy for maintaining majority control of the General Assembly. The judges—two Democrats and a Republican—described themselves as "each hailing from different geographic regions and each with differing ideological and political outlooks." They ruled that the legislative districts violated the "free elections clause of the North Carolina constitution," which "guarantees that all elections must be conducted freely and honestly to ascertain, fairly and truthfully, the will of the people." "It is not the free will of the people that is fairly ascertained through extreme partisan gerrymandering," the judges wrote. "Rather, it is the carefully crafted will of the map drawer that predominates." In late October, the court approved a new, less partisan apportionment scheme for use in the 2020 election. Much will be at stake in that contest. The newly elected lawmakers who gather in Raleigh in 2021 will redraw the legislative map once more, this time on the basis of the 2020 census, and they will no doubt put their mark on state election law.[57]

Two additional losses followed in quick succession, both related to SB 824. Soon after the bill became law, the North Carolina Conference of the NAACP and plaintiffs represented by the Southern Coalition for Social Justice went to court to challenge its constitutionality.

The NAACP case was heard by Judge Loretta Biggs in the U.S. District Court for the Middle District of North Carolina. In December 2019, she enjoined implementation of the photo ID requirement, pending a later trial, on grounds that it was "impermissibly motivated, at least in part, by discriminatory intent." As evidence of that fact, she noted that "the same key legislators who championed HB 589 [in 2013] were the driving force behind SB 824's passage just a few years later."[58]

In February 2020, two months after Biggs's ruling, the North Carolina Appeals Court issued a similar order in the case of the Southern Coalition plaintiffs. A three-judge panel noted that SB 824 specifically disallowed the use of the photo IDs issued to recipients of public assistance, which "were disproportionately possessed by African American voters." "Such a choice," the jurists wrote, "speaks more of an intention to target African American voters rather than a desire to comply with the newly created [constitutional] Amendment in a fair and balanced manner." That was reason enough to conclude that, at trial, the Southern Coalition plaintiffs would likely prevail in their claim that SB 824 violated the North Carolina Constitution's guarantee of equal protection of the laws and prohibition of racial discrimination.[59]

Republican lieutenant governor Dan Forest characterized these injunctions as "baseless decision[s]" handed down by "unelected activist liberal judge[s]." "It's time," he declared, "to restore the rule of law in North Carolina." Allison Riggs, lead counsel for the Southern Coalition plaintiffs, countered that the courts had done just that by blocking a "racially discriminatory" effort to suppress the black vote.[60]

As we approach the 2020 election, the challenges to SB 824 are yet to be resolved—as is the future of North Carolina's fragile democracy.

Conclusion Looking Backward to the Future

The contest over the photo ID amendment is the latest chapter in North Carolina's long and cyclical history of struggle over minority voting rights. Many observers have described the amendment as a "solution in search of a problem." That is a reasonable enough characterization, but it can obscure an important historical lesson. Modern Republican lawmakers are, in fact, seeking to solve a problem—one that has vexed conservatives, regardless of political party, for generations. As political scientist Corey Robin suggests, they are opposed not so much to democracy as to its extension downward. Republican leaders today understand the ramifications of expanded minority political participation. Throughout North Carolina's history, when minority citizens have built alliances with progressive whites and gained access to the ballot box, they have cast their votes to advance an enduring agenda for equal justice, civil rights, and democratic governance. Martin Luther King Jr. captured its substance in a 1961 address to an interracial audience of labor leaders: "decent wages, fair working conditions, livable housing, old age security, health and welfare measures, conditions in which families can grow, have education for their children, and respect in the community." These things, King declared, "shall bring into full realization the American dream—a dream yet unfulfilled. A dream of equality of opportunity, of privilege and property widely distributed; a dream of a land where men will not take necessities from the many to give luxuries to the few . . . a dream of a nation where all our gifts and resources are held not for ourselves alone but as instruments of service for the rest of humanity; the dream of a country where every man will respect the dignity and worth of human personality—that is the dream."[1]

It is no coincidence that recent election-security campaigns in North Carolina erupted in a historical moment marked by record levels of black political participation, the election of the nation's first black president, and growth in Hispanic and immigrant populations that within our lifetimes will make the United States a minority-majority nation. For many white Americans, these developments are the source of a profound sense of loss, a longing for the privileges once associated with skin color, a desire to "make America great again." That is hardly surprising in a nation that from its founding defined white freedom and citizenship rights in ways that necessitated black subjugation, first in slavery and then under the regime of Jim Crow. The human cost of this deceit is too easily tallied. It includes the thousands of North Carolinians who are in poor health but have been denied access to care by lawmakers' refusal to extend the benefits of Medicaid. We see it in under-resourced schools, where children are deprived of a fair start in life. It is evident in the precarious lives of neighbors who are hungry and ill-housed, who without the protection of a strong social safety net are one incident of misfortune away from poverty.

Where, in the face of all of this, are we to find hope? History can be our guide. The stories that fill these pages bear witness to the struggles of North Carolinians who, across many generations, worked to break through the obfuscations of race and establish genuine democracy. They declared their principles at the state constitutional convention of 1868, where they framed a new government instituted "solely for the good of the whole." They declare them still in calls for a new fusion politics founded on an understanding that democracy building begins with a radical commitment to human equality. Like our forebears at other critical moments in our history, we stand at a crossroads. Before us there are two divergent paths into the future. Will we walk toward democracy, or satisfy ourselves with continuing to live in the shadow of slavery and Jim Crow? This is *our* time for choosing.

Acknowledgments

This book began with research for expert witness reports that Jim prepared for two voting rights lawsuits: *North Carolina State Conference of the NAACP v. McCrory*, which was decided for the plaintiffs by the Fourth Circuit Court of Appeals in 2016, and *North Carolina Conference of the NAACP v. Cooper*, which is currently pending in the U.S. District Court for the Middle District of North Carolina. We have been privileged to work on behalf of courageous men and women who demanded their day in court and to learn from attorneys who are deeply committed to principles of equal justice and democratic citizenship. Together, they offered us a challenging opportunity to think about the ways that studying the past can inform some of the most important debates in contemporary American life.

A book represents the labor of many hands. We are grateful to Francesca Prince, who contributed to our research by mining the intricacies of twentieth-century North Carolina election law, and to Kirsten Leloudis, who helped us identify early challenges to disenfranchisement that have been largely overlooked in the legal and historical literature on voting rights. Jacquelyn Hall, Caitlin Swain, Penda Hair, and the legal team at Forward Justice pored over numerous drafts of our work. Their insights sharpened our thinking, as did the incisive commentary we received from anonymous colleagues who read our manuscript for the University of North Carolina Press. We are also deeply indebted to Mark Simpson-Vos, editorial director at UNC Press, who early on saw the value of turning our work on voting rights into a book for the people of North Carolina, and to our copyeditors, Christi Stanforth and Katie Haywood.

As we write these words, we are surrounded by bookshelves laden with the work of our teachers, colleagues, and students. Readers will find many of their names in the bibliography. Over the years, they have sustained us as scholars and taught us how to think about race and democracy in North Carolina, the South, and the nation.

Finally, we owe thanks to our spouses, Dianne Leloudis and Jacquelyn Hall, and to Rebecca Leloudis, who stood by us throughout this project. They are in their own lives and careers fierce champions of justice.

Notes

Introduction

1. "America the Vulnerable"; Waldman, *Fight to Vote*; Levitt, "'Truth about Voter Fraud." For recent scholarship on voting rights, see C. Anderson, *One Person, No Vote*; Berman, *Give Us the Ballot*; and Lichtman, *Embattled Vote in America*. Important earlier studies include S. F. Lawson, *Black Ballots*; Keyssar, *Right to Vote*; and Kousser, *Colorblind Injustice*.

2. *North Carolina State Conference of the NAACP v. McCrory*, Civ. No. 1:13-cv-658, 1. For a complete online collection of documents related to this case, see "North Carolina v. North Carolina NAACP."

3. Purdy, "North Carolina's Long Moral March"; Carmichael, *Lincoln's Gettysburg Address*, 72; "Speech on the Restoration of State Government," January 21, 1864, in Graf and Haskins, *Papers of Andrew Johnson*, 6:577–78; Foner, *Second Founding*.

4. "Address Accepting the Democratic Nomination for Governor, April 11, 1900," Connor and Poe, *Life and Speeches of Charles Brantley Aycock*, 211–27.

Chapter 1

1. Escott, *Many Excellent People*, 15; Orth, "North Carolina Constitutional History," 1772, 1776n114; Jeffrey, "'Free Suffrage' Revisited," 27–28.

2. Kenneth Rayner to Thomas Ruffin, December 25, 1860, in Hamilton, *Papers of Thomas Ruffin*, 3:109; Escott, *Many Excellent People*, 28–30.

3. Helper, *Impending Crisis of the South*, 152–53. Throughout the book, Helper railed at "villainous" slave owners. "Too long have we yielded a submissive obedience to the tyrannical domination of an inflated oligarchy," he declared; "too long have we tolerated their arrogance and self-conceit; too long have we submitted to their unjust and savage exactions. Let us now wrest from them the sceptre of power, establish liberty and equal rights throughout the land, and henceforth and forever guard our legislative halls from the pollutions and usurpations of proslavery demagogues." See pp. 28, 121.

4. *Semi-weekly Standard* (Raleigh, N.C.), January 19, 1864; O. Goddin to Zebulon Vance, February 27, 1863, in Yearns and Barrett, *North Carolina Civil War Documentary*, 98; Escott, *Many Excellent People*, 36, 44, 49,

65–67. On internal dissent during the Civil War, see also Durrill, *War of Another Kind*.

5. Calvin Wiley to Zebulon Vance, January 24, 1865, quoted in Escott, *Many Excellent People*, 89–90; Jasper Spruill to Josiah Collins, April 22, 1863, and Thomas J. Norman to Josiah Collins, June 23, 1863, quoted in Durrill, *War of Another Kind*, 173, 179.

6. William S. Pettigrew to Sir, January 5, 1864, and William S. Pettigrew speech, July 12, 1864, quoted in Durrill, *War of Another Kind*, 185, 214; A. C. Cowles to Isaac Jarratt, December 3, 1865, quoted in Escott, *Many Excellent People*, 130; *Public Laws of the State of North Carolina, Session of 1866*, chap. 40; *Revised Code of North Carolina, 1854*, chap. 107. See also Browning, "North Carolina Black Code."

7. Hamilton, *Papers of Randolph Abbott Shotwell*, 2:231.

8. *Statutes at Large, Treaties, and Proclamations*, 429; Escott, *Many Excellent People*, 135. The law was formally titled An Act to Provide for the More Efficient Government of the Rebel States.

9. Hamilton, *Reconstruction in North Carolina*, 240–50; Owens, "Union League of America," 82–115.

10. Andrews, *South since the War*, 129–30; Escott, *Many Excellent People*, 142; Bernstein, "Participation of Negro Delegates in the Constitutional Convention of 1868," 391.

11. *Constitution of the State of North Carolina, 1868*, art. 5, sec. 2; art. 6, sec. 1; art. 7, sec. 1; art. 11, sec. 7; Orth, "North Carolina Constitutional History," 1779; *Constitution of the State of North Carolina, 1868*, Ordinances, chap. 36.

12. Raper, *William W. Holden*, 101; Foner, *Reconstruction*, 332.

13. *Proceedings of the Colored National Labor Convention*, 4, 11–12; Powell, *Dictionary of North Carolina Biography*, 3:53.

14. Escott, *Many Excellent People*, 145–51; "The Election," *Wilmington (N.C.) Journal*, November 29, 1867; "The Fastidiousness of the Convention," *Wilmington (N.C.) Journal*, January 24, 1868.

15. Foner, *Reconstruction*, 342; Hamilton, *Reconstruction in North Carolina*, 461.

16. A. W. Tourgée to William Holden, July 3, 1869, quoted in Raper, *William W. Holden*, 160; Hamilton, *Papers of Randolph Abbott Shotwell*, 2:376. On Klan violence generally, and the murders of Stephens and Outlaw, see Raper, *William W. Holden*, 155–66; Stedman, *Murder and Mystery*; and Troxler, "'To Look More Closely at the Man.'"

17. Raper, *William W. Holden*, 167–223; Brisson, "'Civil Government Was Crumbling around Me'"; "The Civil Law Triumphant—Military Despotism Overthrown," *Old North State* (Salisbury, N.C.), August 26, 1870.

18. Hamilton, *Reconstruction in North Carolina*, 565–67, 599, 636–42, 654; Orth, "North Carolina Constitutional History," 1781–84; *Amendments to the Constitution of North Carolina, Proposed by the Constitutional Convention of 1875*; Escott, *Many Excellent People*, 166–69; "Communism," *Enquirer* (Tarboro, N.C.), November 25, 1871.

19. Foner, *Reconstruction*, 564–87; Clendenen, "President Hayes' 'Withdrawal' of the Troops"; Woodward, *Reunion and Reaction*.

20. Crow, "Cracking the Solid South," 335; Escott, *Many Excellent People*, 181. On North Carolina's black congressmen, see E. Anderson, *Race and Politics in North Carolina*.

21. Hall et al., *Like a Family*, 5–8; Petty, *Standing Their Ground*, 29–124; Goldfield, *Still Fighting the Civil War*, 277–78.

22. Escott, *Many Excellent People*, 188–90; Durrill, "Producing Poverty"; Petition of Forty-Nine Citizens of Alexander County, February 3, 1879, quoted in Escott, *Many Excellent People*, 190.

23. Hall et al., *Like a Family*, chaps. 1–2; *Tenth Annual Report of the Bureau of Labor Statistics*, 76; Korstad, *Civil Rights Unionism*, 93–98.

24. Beckel, *Radical Reform*, 135–77; "North Carolina Governor, 1892."

25. "Will Men Bolt Their Convictions?," *Caucasian*, March 12, 1896. Republicans won thirty-eight seats in the state house of representatives and eighteen in the state senate; Populists took thirty-six seats in the house and twenty-four in the senate. See Edmonds, *Negro and Fusion Politics*, 37. On the Knights of Labor, see Beckel, *Radical Reform*, 116–28.

26. Kousser, *Shaping of Southern Politics*, 186; *Public Laws and Resolutions of the State of North Carolina, Session of 1895*, chaps. 69, 73, 116, 135, 174, 183, 219, 275, 348.

27. *Public Laws and Resolutions of the State of North Carolina, Session of 1895*, chap. 159, sec. 5; *Public Laws and Resolutions of the State of North Carolina, Session of 1897*, chap. 185, sec. 72.

28. *Public Laws and Resolutions of the State of North Carolina, Session of 1895*, chap. 159, sec. 7.

29. *Public Laws and Resolutions of the State of North Carolina, Session of 1895*, chap. 159, secs. 38, 39, 41.

30. *Public Laws and Resolutions of the State of North Carolina, Session of 1895*, chap. 159, secs. 10–12, 14.

31. *Report of Population of the United States at the Eleventh Census: 1890*, part 2, xxxv; *Public Laws and Resolutions of the State of North Carolina, Session of 1895*, chap. 159, secs. 19–20; Trelease, "Fusion Legislatures of 1895 and 1897," 282; Kousser, *Shaping of Southern Politics*, 190.

32. *Public Laws and Resolutions of the State of North Carolina, Session of 1895*, chap. 159, sec. 72.

33. Beckel, *Radical Reform*, 179–80; Kousser, *Shaping of Southern Politics*, 182. Republicans won fifty-four seats in the state house of representatives and eighteen seats in the state senate; Populists took thirty-nine seats in the house and twenty-five seats in the senate. See Edmonds, *Negro and Fusion Politics*, 59.

34. *Public Laws and Resolutions of the State of North Carolina, Session of 1897*, chap. 421.

35. *Public Laws and Resolutions of the State of North Carolina, Session of 1897*, chap. 108.

36. *Constitution of the State of North Carolina, 1868*, art. 1, secs. 1–2; Kousser, *Shaping of Southern Politics*, 183.

37. Escott, *Many Excellent People*, 253–58; Korstad and Leloudis, *To Right These Wrongs*, 206. On the Black Second, see E. Anderson, *Race and Politics in North Carolina*; and Justesen, *George Henry White*.

38. Korstad, *Civil Rights Unionism*, 53; Prather, "Red Shirt Movement." On Populists' vulnerability to racial appeals, see Edmonds, *Negro and Fusion Politics*, 136.

39. For a detailed account of events in Wilmington, see Umfleet, *Day of Blood*. The book began as *1898 Wilmington Race Riot Report*, commissioned by the state legislature in 2000. In 2007, lawmakers expressed "profound regret that violence, intimidation, and force were used to replace a duly elected local government, that people lost their livelihoods and were forced to leave their homes, and that the government was unsuccessful in protecting its citizens during that time." See Joint Resolution Acknowledging the Findings of the 1898 Wilmington Race Riot Commission.

40. "Defamer Must Go," *News and Observer* (Raleigh, N.C.), November 10, 1898; "Citizens Aroused," *Morning Star* (Wilmington, N.C.), November 10, 1898.

41. Untitled news item, *Charlotte Daily Observer*, June 6, 1900; Escott, *Many Excellent People*, 258.

42. *Laws and Resolutions of the State of North Carolina, Adjourned Session 1900*, chap. 2.

43. *Laws and Resolutions of the State of North Carolina, Adjourned Session 1900*, chap. 2.

44. "Democratic State Senators," *Union Republican* (Winston, N.C.), January 19, 1899; *Public Laws and Resolutions of the State of North Carolina, Session of 1899*, chap. 16.

45. *Public Laws and Resolutions of the State of North Carolina, Session of 1899*, chap. 507, secs. 11, 19.

46. *Public Laws and Resolutions of the State of North Carolina, Session of 1899*, chap. 507, secs. 11, 21, 22.

47. *Public Laws and Resolutions of the State of North Carolina, Session of 1899*, chap. 507, secs. 4, 5, 8, 9.

48. *Public Laws and Resolutions of the State of North Carolina, Session of 1899*, chap. 507, secs. 27, 29.

49. "Aycock at Snow Hill," *Morning Post* (Raleigh, N.C.), March 1, 1900; Connor and Poe, *Life and Speeches of Charles Brantley Aycock*, 82, 218–19, 225.

50. "Aycock at Snow Hill," *Morning Post* (Raleigh, N.C.), March 1, 1900; Prather, "Red Shirt Movement," 181–83; Kousser, *Shaping of Southern Politics*, 193.

51. Untitled item, *Charlotte Daily Observer*, June 6, 1900; Woodward, *Origins of the New South*, 328.

Chapter 2

1. Escott, *Many Excellent People*, 261; Redding, *Making Race, Making Power*, 14.

2. Kousser, *Shaping of Southern Politics*, 261. On Jim Crow as a system of plunder, see Coates, "Case for Reparations." "Plunder," Coates writes, "had been the essential feature of slavery . . . but practically a full century after the end of the Civil War and the abolition of slavery, the plunder—quiet, systemic, submerged—continued."

3. *Public Laws and Resolutions of the State of North Carolina, Session of 1899*, chap. 384; "A Sampling of Jim Crow Laws."

4. Hanchett, *Sorting Out the New South City*, 3, chaps. 1–6.

5. Herbin-Triant, "Southern Segregation South Africa–Style," 171, 179–80.

6. Herbin-Triant, "Southern Segregation South Africa–Style," 181, 186, 188–89.

7. Brown, *Upbuilding Black Durham*, 236, passim; Korstad, *Civil Rights Unionism*, 91, 95–96.

8. Hall et al., *Like a Family*, 24, 29, 31, 80; Wright, *Old South, New South*, 183; Williamson, *Crucible of Race*, 430–32; Du Bois, *Black Reconstruction*, 700.

9. Kousser, "Progressivism—for Middle-Class Whites Only," 178; Thuesen, *Greater Than Equal*, 31, 86, 268n48.

10. National Emergency Council, *Report on Economic Conditions of the South*, 29; Larkins, *Negro Population of North Carolina*, 30; Shin, "Black-White Differentials in Infant Mortality in the South, 1940–1970," 17. The infant mortality rate for blacks was 76.6 per thousand live births, compared to 50.3 per thousand live births for whites.

11. Snider, *Helms and Hunt*; Key, *Southern Politics*, 211–15.

12. Christensen, *Paradox of Tar Heel Politics*, 44; *Good Health Campaign of North Carolina*, 30; Chafe, *Civilities and Civil Rights*, 339.

13. "Republic Cotton Mills," "Lowe Manufacturing Company," "Icemorlee Cotton Mills Co.," and "Munford Cotton Mill Company," *Southern Textile Bulletin*, December 25, 1919, 43, 159, 240, 275; Marion Kiwanis club advertisement quoted in Lewis, *Cheap and Contented Labor*, 31.

14. "White Men to the Front," *Wilmington (N.C.) Messenger*, May 13, 1898; "Mountain People Endorse Morrison's Red Shirt Record," *Union Herald* (Raleigh, N.C.), October 14, 1920; "Hoey Denounces Anti-lynch Bill," *News and Observer* (Raleigh, N.C.), February 17, 1940; speech fragments, series 3, folder 60, Kitchin Papers #04018; "The Governor's Speech," *Public Ledger* (Oxford, N.C.), November 5, 1909.

15. Josephus Daniels to John Temple Graves, December 21, 1942, quoted in Ward, *Defending White Democracy*, 2.

16. Goldenberg, "African-American Troops Fought to Fight in World War I"; Williams, *Torchbearers of Democracy*, 7; "Returning Soldiers," 14.

17. Zogry, "House That Dr. Pope Built," 183–216, quotation at 213.

18. Gilmore, *Gender and Jim Crow*, quotation at 213; "A Challenge to the White Men and Women of North Carolina," *Greensboro (N.C.) Patriot*, September 27, 1920. On the number of black women registrants, see Gilmore, *Gender and Jim Crow*, 223.

19. Estimates of the scale of the Great Migration vary. The figures cited here are from Gregory, "Second Great Migration," 21. On the New Negro, see Whalan, *Great War and the Culture of the New Negro*.

20. Katznelson, *Fear Itself*, 175–76; Sitkoff, *Toward Freedom Land*, 29–36; *Final Report of the WPA Program, 1935–43*, 45, 107; Ladd with Hadley, *Transformations of the American Party System*, 59.

21. "North Carolinians Hold State-wide Political Confab," *Pittsburgh Courier*, April 2, 1932; "Durham, Thriving Southern Metropolis of 17,000 Negro Inhabitants," *Norfolk Journal and Guide*, April 16, 1932; Martin, "Negro Leaders, the Republican Party, and the Election of 1932"; Garcia, "Black Disaffection from the Republican Party," 465–69; Gershenhorn, *Louis Austin*, quotation at p. 31; "Carolina Whites Horrified as Negro Democrats Vote," *Atlanta Daily World*, June 6, 1932.

22. "Dagger at the Heart," *News and Observer* (Raleigh, N.C.), May 25, 1932; "More Talk about Negro Situation," *News and Observer* (Raleigh, N.C.), June 1, 1932; Gershenhorn, *Louis Austin*, 49.

23. "North Carolina Brings Out Vote," *Indianapolis Recorder*, November 14, 1936; Gershenhorn, "Courageous Voice for Black Freedom," 82–84. Gershenhorn pegs the upper voter registration number at fifty thousand.

24. "Elect Magistrates on Democratic Ticket in North Carolina," *Pittsburgh Courier*, November 24, 1934.

25. *Congressional Record* 82: 1938; Bailey to R. G. Cherry, March 1, 1938, quoted in Patterson, "Failure of Party Realignment in the South," 603; Bailey to Peter Gerry, October 25, 1937, quoted in J. R. Moore, "Senator Josiah W. Bailey and the 'Conservative Manifesto' of 1937."

26. Josiah Bailey to James Farley, October 3, 1938, quoted in Milkis, "New Deal," 88–89.

27. Katznelson, *Fear Itself*, chap. 5; Badger, *North Carolina and the New Deal*, 47. See also Abrams, *Conservative Constraints*.

28. Guy B. Johnson, "Does the South Owe the Negro a New Deal?"

29. Dalfiume, "'Forgotten Years' of the Negro Revolution," 99–100; Zieger, *CIO*.

30. Jones, *March on Washington*, chap. 1.

31. Korstad, *Civil Rights Unionism*, 202.

32. Korstad, *Civil Rights Unionism*, 251–52, 306–10.

33. On Wallace's life and career, see Culver and Hyde, *American Dreamer*.

34. "Wallace Party Names Picks for N.C. Posts," *Norfolk Journal and Guide*, September 4, 1948; "Report of the Nominating Committee, Progressive Party of North Carolina," box 2, folder 13, Scales Papers #4879. On Blackwell, see Chafe, *Civilities and Civil Rights*, 27–28. For more on the Progressive Party and the Wallace campaign in North Carolina, see Uesugi, "Gender, Race, and the Cold War."

35. Devine, *Henry Wallace's 1948 Presidential Campaign*, 245; "Deplorable Disorders," *Charlotte Observer*, September 1, 1948.

36. Wallace, "Ten Extra Years."

37. Wallace, "Ten Extra Years."

38. Christensen, *Paradox of Tar Heel Politics*, 115; "Scott Trades Verbal Blows with His Foe," *Gastonia Gazette*, June 24, 1948, quoted in Christensen, *Rise and Fall of the Branchhead Boys*, 37. On infrastructure, see Christensen, *Rise and Fall of the Branchhead Boys*, 52–62, 64–70.

39. "Jesse Helms and Senator at Odds in Many Matters Get Together," *Daily Times-News*, February 13, 1957, quoted in Christensen, *Rise and Fall of the Branchhead Boys*, 36–37.

40. Christensen, *Paradox of Tar Heel Politics*, 115; "Scott Pledges Negro Program," *News and Observer* (Raleigh, N.C.), January 15, 1949. On the right-to-work law and Trigg's appointment, see Christensen, *Rise and Fall of the Branchhead Boys*, 70–72.

41. Pleasants and Burns, *Frank Porter Graham and the 1950 Senate Race*, 5–30; Ashby, *Frank Porter Graham*, 77, 144–45, 151–59.

42. Griffin interview; "Group of Business Men Forms State Association," *News and Observer* (Raleigh, N.C.), December 12, 1942; Wills, "Stockton, Richard Gordon"; "Personal Profile: Edwin Pate."

43. "Comparisons Are Certain for Citizens' Association," *News and Observer* (Raleigh, N.C.), December 13, 1942; Goldstein, "American Liberty League"; Jenkins, *Hoods and Shirts*, 59; Patton, "Standing at Thermopylae."

44. "North Carolinians Must Assume Personal Responsibility for Our Low Per Capita Income," *Congressional Record* 101, part 9, 11934, 11938; "Kerr Scott: Man of Surprise, Controversy," *News and Observer* (Raleigh, N.C.), January 4, 1953; "Vox Populi," *News and Observer* (Raleigh, N.C.), May 17, 1949.

45. Ashby, *Frank Porter Graham*, 258, 261–62; Pleasants and Burns, *Frank Porter Graham and the 1950 Senate Race*, 96–97, 174–76, 186.

46. Pleasants and Burns, *Frank Porter Graham and the 1950 Senate Race*, 196–201; Griffin interview.

47. President's Committee on Civil Rights, *To Secure These Rights*, 166.

48. Campaign handbills, folders 145–46, Powell Papers #04364.

49. Campaign handbills, folders 145–46, Powell Papers #04364; Ashby, *Frank Porter Graham*, 267.

50. Pleasants and Burns, *Frank Porter Graham and the 1950 Senate Race*, 244.

51. WKS radio address, June 20, 1950, quoted in Christensen, *Rise and Fall of the Branchhead Boys*, 87; Jonathan Daniels, "Political Arson," *News and Observer* (Raleigh, N.C.), June 18, 1950.

Chapter 3

1. Lillian Turner to Frank Graham, June 26, 1950, quoted in Pleasants and Burns, *Frank Porter Graham and the 1950 Senate Race*, 247–48; "Victorious in Defeat," *Carolina Times* (Durham, N.C.), July 1, 1950.

2. "Rush of Negro Candidates for City Posts in N. Carolina," *Atlanta Daily World*, May 8, 1951; "Two Win City Council Seats in No. Carolina," *Atlanta Daily World*, May 17, 1951; "First Negro to N.C. League of Municipalities," *Atlanta Daily World*, November 10, 1951. William Hampton won election to the Greensboro city council; Reverend William R. Crawford won a runoff to fill Kenneth Williams's empty seat on the Winston-Salem board of aldermen; and W. P. Devane was reelected to the Fayetteville city council. Later in 1951, Hampton and Crawford were the first black city officials to attend meetings of the North Carolina League of Municipalities.

3. "Negro Candidates Seek Offices in Twenty North Carolina Cities,"

Chicago Defender, May 2, 1953. Despite the title, only nineteen cities are listed in this article. For clarification on the number of city council candidates in Concord, see "Candidates Win Three North Carolina Races," *Atlanta Daily World*, May 7, 1953; and "Primary Vote at Concord Slated Tuesday," *Charlotte Observer*, April 13, 1953. For the successful candidates, see "They Scored," *Chicago Defender*, May 23, 1953. William Crawford and William Hampton won reelection in Winston-Salem and Greensboro, respectively; Rencher N. Harris claimed a seat on the Durham city council; Hubert J. Robinson was elected to the Chapel Hill town council; Nathaniel Barber took a seat on the city council in Gastonia; and George K. Butterfield Sr. was elected to the city council in Wilson.

4. Gershenhorn, *Louis Austin*, 114; "They Scored," *Chicago Defender*, May 23, 1953.

5. McKinney, *Greater Freedom*, 21–22, 54; Butterfield interview.

6. McKinney, *Greater Freedom*, 58–59; Butterfield interview.

7. McKinney, *Greater Freedom*, 91–96; Butterfield interview.

8. *Session Laws and Resolutions, State of North Carolina, Extra Session of 1956, and Regular Session, 1957*, chap. 13.

9. McKinney, *Greater Freedom*, 96, 139–44; Butterfield interview; *Watkins v. City of Wilson*, 121 S.E.2d 861 (N.C. 1961); *Watkins v. Wilson*, 370 U.S. 46 (1962).

10. "Failure of Singleshot Ban May Strengthen Black Vote," *News and Observer* (Raleigh, N.C.), January 17, 1972.

11. *News and Observer* (Raleigh, N.C.), June 22, 1950.

12. "The 'Negro Bloc' and the 'Single Shot,'" *Carolina Times* (Durham, N.C.), May 22, 1965.

13. Wertheimer, *Law and Society in the South*, 131–32.

14. Wertheimer, *Law and Society in the South*, chap. 7; D. L. Nixon, "Integration of UNC-Chapel Hill—Law School First." For the following account of Walker's career and legal challenges to Jim Crow election law, we draw broadly on Wertheimer, *Law and Society in the South*; and Barksdale, "Indigenous Civil Rights Movement."

15. Wertheimer, *Law and Society in the South*, 134, 142, 150.

16. Wertheimer, *Law and Society in the South*, 146, 148.

17. Eure, *Public School Laws of North Carolina*, 13–14; *Session Laws and Resolutions, State of North Carolina, Extra Session of 1956, and Regular Session, 1957*, chap. 137; *Walker v. Moss*, 97 S. E.2d 836 (N.C. 1957).

18. North Carolina Advisory Committee to the United States Commission on Civil Rights, *Equal Protection of the Laws in North Carolina*, 28, 33; Wertheimer, *Law and Society in the South*, 141, 151.

19. Public Law 85-315: An Act to Provide Means of Further Securing and Protecting the Civil Rights of Persons within the Jurisdiction of the United States, 637; Winquist, "Civil Rights."

20. *Session Laws and Resolutions, State of North Carolina, Extra Session of 1956, and Regular Session, 1957*, chap. 287; *Lassiter v. Taylor*, 152 F. Supp. 295 (E.D.N.C. 1957).

21. "Defendant Appellee's Brief," *Lassiter v. Northampton Board of Education*, Supreme Court of North Carolina, fall term 1957, no. 172, Sixth District, quoted in Wertheimer, *Law and Society in the South*, 155; *Lassiter v. Northampton County Board of Elections*, 102 S.E.2d 853 (N.C. 1958).

22. *Lassiter v. Northampton County Board of Elections*, 360 U.S. 45 (1959).

23. North Carolina Advisory Committee to the United States Commission on Civil Rights, *Equal Protection of the Laws in North Carolina*, 144; Collins and Margo, "Historical Perspectives on Racial Differences in Schooling," 4.

24. *Bazemore v. Bertie County Board of Elections*, 119 S.E.2d 637 (N.C. 1961).

25. *Bazemore v. Bertie County Board of Elections*, 119 S.E.2d 637 (N.C. 1961); Wertheimer, *Law and Society in the South*, 161; North Carolina Advisory Committee to the United States Commission on Civil Rights, "Voting and Voter Registration in North Carolina, 1960," 22.

26. *Bazemore v. Bertie County Board of Elections*, 119 S.E.2d 637 (N.C. 1961).

27. Towe, *Barriers to Black Political Participation*, 11–12.

28. Thuesen, *Greater Than Equal*, 142–48.

29. Thuesen, *Greater Than Equal*, 147.

30. *Allison v. Sharp*, 184 S.E. 27 (N.C. 1936). On Justice Clarkson, see *Prominent People of North Carolina*, 16–17. In 1896, Clarkson organized one of the state's first "White Supremacy" clubs. Governor Charles Aycock rewarded his political loyalty with an appointment as solicitor of the state's Twelfth Judicial District.

31. Thuesen, *Greater Than Equal*, 151.

32. *Alston v. School Board of City of Norfolk*, 112 F.2d 992 (4th Cir. 1940); Douglas, *Reading, Writing, and Race*, 20; Thuesen, *Greater Than Equal*, 153–55.

33. Thuesen, *Greater Than Equal*, 168–69, 181.

34. *Blue v. Durham Public School District*, 95 F. Supp. 441 (M.D.N.C. 1951).

35. Thuesen, *Greater Than Equal*, 191, 194–95.

36. Thuesen, *Greater Than Equal*, 199; *Brown v. Board of Education of Topeka*, 347 U.S. 483 (1954).

37. *Report of the North Carolina Advisory Committee on Education, April 5, 1956*, 7, 9.

38. *Session Laws and Resolutions, State of North Carolina, 1955*, chap. 366.

39. *Report of the North Carolina Advisory Committee on Education, April 5, 1956*, 8–10; Wettach, "North Carolina School Legislation, 1956"; Batchelor, *Race and Education in North Carolina*, 108–9. The U.S. District Court for the Western District of North Carolina struck down the voucher plan in 1966 (Batchelor, *Race and Education in North Carolina*, 110).

40. Batchelor, *Race and Education in North Carolina*, 73; Chafe, *Civilities and Civil Rights*, 97, 106.

41. Korstad, *Civil Rights Unionism*, 384.

Chapter 4

1. Chafe, *Civilities and Civil Rights*, 99.

2. "Brief of Harry McMullan, Attorney General of North Carolina, Amicus Curiae," 3, 6; *Brown v. Board of Education*, 349 U.S. 294 (1955).

3. "Private Schools Urged for North Carolina," *News and Observer* (Raleigh, N.C.), July 14, 1955; "N.C. Bar Association Award Carries Legacy of Explicit Racism," *News and Observer* (Raleigh, N.C.), June 18, 2016.

4. Covington and Ellis, *Terry Sanford*, chap. 5.

5. Drescher, *Triumph of Good Will*, 67.

6. Drescher, *Triumph of Good Will*, 170–71, 175.

7. Drescher, *Triumph of Good Will*, 94, 218, 297n; Gershenhorn, *Louis Austin*, 171.

8. Manuscript containing notes for an abandoned book on Terry Sanford's term as governor, subseries 3.1, box 174, Records and Papers of Terry Sanford.

9. Wheeler to Sanford, April 29, 1961, quoted in Winford, *John Hervey Wheeler*, 168.

10. Covington and Ellis, *Terry Sanford*, 290; "Commission on Secondary Schools of Southern Association of Colleges and Schools," November 28, 1962, in M. F. Mitchell, *Messages, Addresses, and Public Papers of Terry Sanford*, 301–7.

11. Drescher, *Triumph of Good Will*, 262; "Observations for a Second Century," in manuscript containing notes for an abandoned book on Terry Sanford's term as governor, subseries 3.1, box 174, Records and Papers of Terry Sanford.

12. "Observations for a Second Century," in manuscript containing notes for an abandoned book on Terry Sanford's term as governor, subseries 3.1, box 174, Records and Papers of Terry Sanford; film of Sanford's address to the North Carolina Press Association, series 6.2, VT3531/1a,

Sanford Papers #3531. On Wallace's gubernatorial inauguration, see Carter, *Politics of Rage*, 104–9.

13. "Fraternity's Award Goes to Sanford," *Greensboro (N.C.) Daily News*, April 28, 1963; "A Message to the Negro," in Connor and Poe, *Life and Speeches of Charles Brantley Aycock*, 249–50.

14. Korstad and Leloudis, *To Right These Wrongs*, 57–58, 175.

15. Korstad and Leloudis, *To Right These Wrongs*, 1–2, 87, 111–19, 198.

16. Korstad and Leloudis, *To Right These Wrongs*, 94–107, 109–63.

17. Korstad and Leloudis, *To Right These Wrongs*, 148, 151–54, 158–59, 202–5, 275–81.

18. Kornegay interview; Campbell, *Senator Sam Ervin*, 133, 146.

19. *Civil Rights Acts of 1957, 1960, 1964, 1968, and Voting Rights Act of 1965*, 15–43.

20. Diane Sasson interview, cited in Korstad and Leloudis, *To Right These Wrongs*, 163.

21. Johnson, quoted in Ashmore, *Civil Rights and Wrongs*, 174; W. H. Lawson, *No Small Thing*, 151–59.

22. Combs, *From Selma to Montgomery*, 35–41; Johnson, "President Johnson's Special Message."

23. Johnson, "President Johnson's Special Message."

24. Johnson, "President Johnson's Special Message."

25. *Civil Rights Acts of 1957, 1960, 1964, 1968, and Voting Rights Act of 1965*, 44–53; Laney, *Voting Rights Act of 1965*, 13–24. The following North Carolina counties were originally covered by the Voting Rights Act: Anson, Beaufort, Bertie, Bladen, Camden, Caswell, Chowan, Cleveland, Craven, Cumberland, Edgecombe, Franklin, Gaston, Gates, Granville, Greene, Guilford, Halifax, Harnett, Hertford, Hoke, Lee, Lenoir, Martin, Nash, Northampton, Onslow, Pasquotank, Perquimans, Person, Pitt, Robeson, Rockingham, Scotland, Union, Vance, Wake, Washington, Wayne, and Wilson. Jackson County was added to the list in 1975, and Wake County was removed in 1984.

26. Korstad and Leloudis, *To Right These Wrongs*, 188.

27. Korstad and Leloudis, *To Right These Wrongs*, 190–91.

28. Korstad and Leloudis, *To Right These Wrongs*, 208–25, quotation at 214.

29. North Carolina Voter Education Project, "North Carolina Voter Education Project" (brochure).

30. North Carolina Voter Education Project, *Know Your Voting Rights*; Faulkenbury, *Poll Power*, 99.

31. Phillips, *Emerging Republican Majority*, 325–26.

32. *Drum v. Seawell*, 249 F. Supp. 877 (M.D.N.C. 1965); O'Connor, "Reapportionment and Redistricting," 32–33.

33. *Drum v. Seawell*, 249 F. Supp. 877 (M.D.N.C. 1965). On the principle of one man, one vote, see *Baker v. Carr*, 369 U.S. 186 (1962); *Reynolds v. Sims*, 377 U.S. 533 (1964); and *Wesberry v. Sanders*, 376 U.S. 1 (1964).

34. *Session Laws and Resolutions, State of North Carolina, Extra Session, 1966*, chaps. 1, 5; *Session Laws of the State of North Carolina, Regular Session, 1965*, 9–11.

35. *Session Laws and Resolutions, State of North Carolina, Regular Session, 1967*, chap. 640.

36. *Session Laws and Resolutions, State of North Carolina, Regular Session, 1967*, chap. 1063.

37. "Seat Numbering Bill Produced Hot Debate," *News and Observer* (Raleigh, N.C.), July 8, 1967; "Senate Endorses 'Numbered Seats,'" *News and Observer* (Raleigh, N.C.), July 30, 1967; "Numbered Seat Bill Advances," *News and Observer* (Raleigh, N.C.), June 22, 1967; "Numbered Seats Measure Given House Approval," *News and Observer* (Raleigh, N.C.), June 13, 1967; Towe, *Barriers to Black Political Participation*, 28; *National Roster of Black Elected Officials*; "The Negro Vote," *Greensboro (N.C.) Daily News*, November 11, 1968; "Failure of Singleshot Ban May Strengthen Black Vote," *News and Observer* (Raleigh, N.C.), January 17, 1972.

38. *Session Laws and Resolutions, State of North Carolina, Regular Session, 1971*, chaps. 483, 1177, 1234, 1237; Towe, *Barriers to Black Political Participation*, 61–62; Manderson, "Review of the Patterns and Practices of Racial Discrimination," 31; Watson, "North Carolina Redistricting Process, 1965–1966," 8; *Dunston v. Scott*, 336 F. Supp. 206 (E.D.N.C. 1972).

39. *Dunston v. Scott*, 336 F. Supp. 206 (E.D.N.C. 1972).

40. "North Carolina African-American Legislators, 1969–2019."

41. Keech and Sistrom, "Implementation of the Voting Rights Act in North Carolina," 14.

42. Keech and Sistrom, "Implementation of the Voting Rights Act in North Carolina"; *Gingles v. Edmisten*, 590 F. Supp. 345 (E.D.N.C. 1984).

43. "North Carolina African-American Legislators, 1969–2019"; Earls, Wynes, and Quatrucci, "Voting Rights in North Carolina," 581; "Two Blacks Join N.C.'s U.S. House Delegation," *News and Observer* (Raleigh, N.C.), November 4, 1992; Keech and Sistrom, "Implementation of the Voting Rights Act in North Carolina," 14–17.

44. Kousser, *Colorblind Injustice*, 243–76.

45. N. M. Moore, *Governing Race*, 60; "Goldwater Says He'd Curb Court, Also Stresses States' Rights in Swing through South," *New York Times*,

September 16, 1964; Alsop, "Can Goldwater Win in 64?," 24; Schreiber, "'Where the Ducks Are,'" 157.

46. Morgan, *Reagan*, quotation at 93; "'Welfare Queen' Becomes Issue in Reagan Campaign," *New York Times*, February 15, 1976; Cannon, *President Reagan*, 457–58; Reagan, "A Time for Choosing Address."

47. "1964 Presidential General Election Results—North Carolina."

48. DeLapp to James Gardner, September 1, 1965, box 9; Republican Party in North Carolina, box 16; and DeLapp to William E. Miller, June 6, 1963, box 7, DeLapp Papers.

49. On the purge, see "Negroes Lose Fight in North Carolina," *New York Times*, February 17, 1903.

50. Korstad and Leloudis, *To Right These Wrongs*, 292–93.

51. Korstad and Leloudis, *To Right These Wrongs*, 292–93.

52. Esty, "North Carolina Republicans and the Conservative Revolution," 14–19; "James Gardner Makes Spirited Bid to Take House Seat for Republicans," *News and Observer* (Raleigh, N.C.), May 24, 1964; "Gardner Leaps to GOP Front Rank," *News and Observer* (Raleigh, N.C.), November 9, 1966.

53. Korstad and Leloudis, *To Right These Wrongs*, quotations at 297, 303.

54. Korstad and Leloudis, *To Right These Wrongs*, 297–98.

55. Korstad and Leloudis, *To Right These Wrongs*, quotations at 299, 302.

56. Korstad and Leloudis, *To Right These Wrongs*, quotations at 302.

57. Perlstein, *Nixonland*, 283–85; R. M. Nixon, "Nomination Acceptance Address," August 8, 1968; "1968 Presidential General Election Results—North Carolina."

58. Viewpoint, December 5, 1966, Jesse Helms Viewpoint editorials.

59. Link, *Righteous Warrior*, 144–46, quotation at 9.

60. Pearce, *Jim Hunt*, 11–41; Christensen, *Rise and Fall of the Branchhead Boys*, 232–33.

61. Pearce, *Jim Hunt*, 145–46.

62. Link, *Righteous Warrior*, 268; Kellam, "Helms, Hunt, and Whiteness," 53.

63. Kellam, "Helms, Hunt, and Whiteness," 53; Link, *Righteous Warrior*, 262–69.

64. Link, *Righteous Warrior*, 274, 284; Goldsmith, "Thomas Farr, Jesse Helms, and the Return of the Segregationists."

65. Link, *Righteous Warrior*, 290–91, 304; "Pro-Helms Newspaper Publishes Rumor That Hunt Had a Gay Lover," *News and Observer* (Raleigh, N.C.), July 6, 1984; "Article Stirs New Charges in Carolina Senate Race," *New York Times*, July 7, 1984.

66. Gantt interview.

67. Gantt interview; *Gantt v. Clemson Agricultural College of South Carolina*, 320 F.2d 611 (4th Cir. 1963).

68. Link, *Righteous Warrior*, 375.

69. Goldsmith, "Thomas Farr, Jesse Helms, and the Return of the Segregationists"; Helms, Hands ad; "President Vetoes Bill on Job Rights; Showdown Is Set," *New York Times*, October 23, 1990.

70. Link, *Righteous Warrior*, 380; Earls, Wynes, and Quatrucci, "Voting Rights in North Carolina," 589; Christensen, *Paradox of Tar Heel Politics*, 278.

Chapter 5

1. Christensen, *Paradox of Tar Heel Politics*, 257.

2. Pearce, *Jim Hunt*, 210, quotations at 217, 220.

3. Pearce, *Jim Hunt*, 233–36 (quotation at 234), 263–66; Christensen, *Paradox of Tar Heel Politics*, 241–42. In 1999, Hunt elevated Henry Frye to chief justice of the North Carolina Supreme Court.

4. Berman, *Give Us the Ballot*, 290–91.

5. For increases in black voter registration and turnout, see *North Carolina State Conference of the NAACP v. McCrory*, No. 16-1468 (4th Cir. 2016), 13; Berman, *Give Us the Ballot*, 291.

6. The terms "Hispanic" and "Latino" are often used interchangeably to describe immigrants from Mexico, Cuba, and Central and South America. We use "Hispanic" here and elsewhere because it is the term most often employed by the U.S. Census Bureau, the North Carolina State Board of Elections, other government agencies, and researchers to characterize voters who have ties to those regions.

7. Ross, "Number of Latino Registered Voters Doubles in North Carolina"; "North Carolina's Hispanic Community: 2019 Snapshot"; "Latinos in the 2016 Election: North Carolina."

8. "North Carolina's Hispanic Community: 2019 Snapshot"; Tippett, "Potential Voters Are Fastest-Growing Segment of N.C. Hispanic Population."

9. C. Anderson, *White Rage*, 138–39; "2008 Democratic Party Platform"; "As Republican Convention Emphasizes Diversity, Racial Incidents Intrude," *Washington Post*, August 29, 2012.

10. Gitterman, Coclanis, and Quinterno, "Recession and Recovery in North Carolina," 7; Semuels, "Never-Ending Foreclosure"; "N.C. Foreclosures Jumped 9% in 2008," *Triad Business Journal*, January 5, 2009.

11. "Easley Testifies to State Board of Elections."

12. Mayer, "Covert Operations."

13. Blake, "What Black America Won't Miss about Obama"; "Racial Re-

sentment Adds to GOP Voter Enthusiasm"; Okun, *Emperor Has No Clothes*, 151; Charlotte-Mecklenburg Board of Education, meeting minutes, September 8, 2009; "GOP Mailing Depicts Obama on Food Stamps, Not Dollar Bill"; "'Hanging Obama' Truck Makes Way into Charlotte."

14. Unz, "Immigration, the Republicans, and the End of White America."

15. Mayer, "State for Sale."

16. Mayer, "State for Sale"; "2019 Annual Report," 5.

17. Sturgis, "How Art Pope Helped Turn Back the Clock on Voting Rights in North Carolina"; Bailey, "Gaps in Voter Registration Process." See also Kromm, "Art Pope Bankrolls Dubious 'Voter Fraud' Crusade."

18. Mayer, "State for Sale"; *Citizens United v. Federal Election Commission*, 558 U.S. 310 (2010); *Speechnow.org v. FEC*, No. 08-5223 (D.C. Cir. 2010).

19. Kromm, "Art Pope's Big Day."

20. Roth, *Great Suppression*, 96–98; "GOP Featured McCollum in 2010 Attack Ad."

21. "GOP Featured McCollum in 2010 Attack Ad"; Mayer, "State for Sale"; "Flier Opens an Old Wound," *Winston-Salem (N.C.) Journal*, October 21, 2010; "DNA Evidence Clears Two Men in 1983 Murder," *New York Times*, September 2, 2014.

22. Mixon, "Just Look at the Results," "Narco Gangs in North Carolina," and "Who Benefits from Illegal Immigration?"

23. "Anti-Heagerty Ads: We Just Threw Up in Our Mouths."

24. Millhiser, "Cracks in the GOP's Gerrymandering Firewall." North Carolina's state constitution requires legislative redistricting every ten years, based on the decennial federal census. On REDMAP, see Newkirk, "How Redistricting Became a Technological Arms Race."

25. "Inside the Republican Creation of the North Carolina Voting Bill Dubbed the 'Monster' Law," *Washington Post*, September 2, 2016. For the text of the law, see House Bill 589.

26. Herron and Smith, "Race, *Shelby County*, and the Voter Information Verification Act in North Carolina," 497.

27. *United States v. North Carolina*, 1:13CV861 (M.D.N.C. Feb. 6, 2014); Heberlig, Francia, and Greene, "Conditional Party Teams," 117. In 2008, blacks constituted 21.6 percent of North Carolina's total population. That figure remains unchanged today.

28. Herron and Smith, "Race, *Shelby County*, and the Voter Information Verification Act in North Carolina," 505.

29. Broockman and Roeder, "Hispanics Are the Future of Progressive Strength in America"; Tippett, "North Carolina Hispanics and the Electorate." See also "Republicans Have a Major Demographic Problem, and It's Only Going to Get Worse," *Washington Post*, April 22, 2014; "The South

Is Solidly Republican Right Now; It Might Not Be That Way in 10 Years," *Washington Post*, April 29, 2014; "Immigration Is Changing the Political Landscape in Key States."

30. "Looking, Very Closely, for Voter Fraud," *New York Times*, September 17, 2012; "Madison Project Launches the Code Red USA Project"; Riley, "Lesson from North Carolina on Challenges."

31. Berman, *Give Us the Ballot*, 290.

32. "North Carolina's 2013 Legislative Session Recap"; "NC GOP Rolls Back Era of Democratic Laws," *News and Observer* (Raleigh, N.C.), June 16, 2013.

33. Kotch and Mosteller, "Racial Justice Act," 2035, 2088; "North Carolina Repeals Law Allowing Racial Bias Claim in Death Penalty Challenges," *New York Times*, June 5, 2013; Grosso and O'Brien, "Stubborn Legacy," 1533; Florsheim, "Four Inmates Might Return to Death Row"; "McCrory Signs Repeal of Racial Justice Act," *Winston-Salem (N.C.) Journal*, June 20, 2013; "North Carolina Repeals Law Allowing Racial Bias Claim in Death Penalty Challenges," *New York Times*, June 5, 2013.

34. "Legislation Would Repeal N.C. Tax Credit for Low- and Moderate-Income Taxpayers," *News and Observer* (Raleigh, N.C.), February 14, 2013; T. Mitchell, "North Carolina's Earned Income Tax Credit."

35. Session Law 2013-2, House Bill 4, An Act to Address the Unemployment Insurance Debt, General Assembly of North Carolina; "N.C. Ranks Last among States in Unemployment Benefits," *News and Observer* (Raleigh, N.C.), February 8, 2018.

36. Garfield and Damico, "Coverage Gap," 8; Ku et al., *Economic and Employment Costs of Not Expanding Medicaid*; Dickman et al., "Opting Out of Medicaid Expansion."

37. "Supreme Court Ruling Brings Medicaid Expansion for N.C. into Focus."

38. "North Carolina's Step-by-Step War on Public Education," *Washington Post*, August 7, 2015; Johnson and Ellinwood, *Smart Money*; "2013–2015 North Carolina Budget Short-Changes Students, Teachers, and Public Education."

39. "NCAE Wins Challenge to Payroll Dues Ban"; Gerhardt, "Pay Our Teachers or Lose Your Job"; Wagner, "North Carolina Once Again toward the Bottom in National Rankings on Teacher Pay"; Johnson and Ellinwood, *Smart Money*; Brenneman, "Teacher Attrition Continues to Plague North Carolina."

40. "2013–14 School Performance Grades (A–F) for North Carolina Public Schools." On the grading scheme, see *Unraveling*.

41. Ladd, Clotfelter, and Holbein, "Growing Segmentation of the Char-

ter School Sector in North Carolina," 11, 35; "White Parents in North Carolina Are Using Charter Schools to Secede from the Education System," *Washington Post*, April 15, 2015.

42. *School Vouchers in North Carolina*, 1–2, 7, 11–13, 21n2; "Opportunity Scholarship Program, 2019–20 School Year"; "Private School Minority Statistics in North Carolina."

43. "North Carolina's 'Racial Justice Act'"; "Berger and Moore Celebrate Majority Victory in State Legislature," *News and Observer* (Raleigh, N.C.), updated February 9, 2018.

44. *North Carolina State Conference of the NAACP v. McCrory*, No. 16-1468 (4th Cir. 2016), 46; Sirota, "Income Tax Rate Cap Amendment Is Costly to Taxpayers, Communities"; Sirota, "Public Investment Falls, Tax Responsibility Shifts"; "In N.C., Tax Cuts Widen Income Inequality," *News and Observer* (Raleigh, N.C.), April 26, 2019; "Voters Lower Cap on Income Taxes in North Carolina."

45. Barber, *Third Reconstruction*, ix–xvi; Rawls, "Liberal Protest That Would Shock the Right"; Blest, "Over 80,000 People Joined the Biggest-Ever Moral March in North Carolina"; "Understanding HB2: North Carolina's Newest Law Solidifies State's Role in Defining Discrimination," *Charlotte Observer*, March 26, 2016.

46. Sturgis, "Art Pope–Funded Group Launches Database Targeting Moral Monday Arrestees"; "Circus Goes On."

47. *North Carolina State Conference of the NAACP v. McCrory*, Civ No. 1:13-cv-658, 7–10.

48. *North Carolina State Conference of the NAACP v. McCrory*, 182 F. Supp. 3d 320 (M.D.N.C. 2016).

49. *North Carolina State Conference of the NAACP v. McCrory*, No. 16-1468 (4th Cir. 2016), 9–11, 77–78; "Voting Rights—Judges Throw Out N.C.'s Voter ID Law," *News and Observer* (Raleigh, N.C.), July 30, 2016.

50. "McCrory Asks Supreme Court to Restore Voter ID Law," *News and Observer* (Raleigh, N.C.), August 16, 2016; "N.C. Republican Party Seeks 'Party Line Changes' to Limit Early Voting Hours," *News and Observer* (Raleigh, N.C.), August 18, 2016.

51. Newkirk, "What Early Voting in North Carolina Actually Reveals"; "NCGOP Sees Encouraging Early Voting, Obama/Clinton Coalition Tire/Fail to Resonate in North Carolina."

52. *North Carolina v. North Carolina State Conference of the NAACP*, 137 S. Ct. 1399 (2017).

53. "Supreme Court Won't Rescue N.C. Voter ID Law; GOP Leaders Say They Will Try Again with New Law," *News and Observer* (Raleigh, N.C.), May 15, 2017; An Act to Amend the North Carolina Constitution to Require

Photo Identification to Vote in Person, S.L. 2018-128, H.B. 1092; "Voter ID to Go on N.C. Ballots."

54. "Voter ID: A Form of Suppression or Necessary Protection?"; "Support Voter ID Today"; "Voter ID Is Back in North Carolina, and the Justifications Are as Lame as Ever," *Charlotte Observer*, June 7, 2018; "North Carolina Voter ID Amendment Debate Features Misleading Claims."

55. "Citizens without Proof," 3; Schofield, "County-by-County Data Reveal Dramatic Impact of Proposed Election Changes on Voters"; Atkeson et al., "New Barriers to Participation"; *Postelection Audit Report: General Election 2016*, appendix 4.2; "Voter ID Is Back in North Carolina, and the Justifications Are as Lame as Ever," *Charlotte Observer*, June 7, 2018; "North Carolina Voter ID Amendment Debate Features Misleading Claims"; American Express Merchant Reference Guide—U.S.; Visa Core Rules and Visa Product and Services Rules; Mastercard Transaction Processing Rules, 75.

56. "North Carolina Voter ID Amendment (2018)"; "Support Voter ID Today." Woodhouse's comments are transcribed from a video recording of a press conference he held on July 29, 2016. See "N.C. Voter ID Law Overturned."

57. "N.C. Gerrymandering: Legislature Lines Ruled Unconstitutional," *News and Observer* (Raleigh, N.C.), September 3, 2019; "North Carolina's Legislative Maps Are Thrown Out by State Court Panel," *New York Times*, September 3, 2019; "New Maps Ordered for N.C. 2020 Congressional Races, in Win for Democrats," *News and Observer* (Raleigh, N.C.), October 28, 2019.

58. Boughton, "N.C. Voter ID Law Written with 'Discriminatory Intent,' Says Judge Who Blocked It," *News and Observer* (Raleigh, N.C.), December 31, 2019; *North Carolina State Conference of the NAACP v. Cooper*, 1:18CV1034 (M.D.N.C. Dec. 31, 2019).

59. Boughton, "N.C. Court of Appeals Throws Out Voter Photo ID for Now"; *Holmes v. Moore*, COA19-762 (Feb. 18, 2020).

60. Forest, Twitter posts; Riggs, Twitter post.

Conclusion

1. Robin, *Reactionary Mind*, 8–9; McGaughey, *Casebook on Labour Law*, 33–34.

Bibliography

Archival Sources
Chapel Hill, North Carolina
   Wilson Library, University of North Carolina
      North Carolina Collection
         Jesse Helms Viewpoint editorial transcripts,
            C384.5 H48v nos. 1001–1750
      Southern Historical Collection
         William W. Kitchin Papers #4018
         Daniel Augustus Powell Papers #4364
         Terry Sanford Papers #3531
         Junius Irving Scales Papers #4879
Durham, North Carolina
   David M. Rubenstein Rare Book and Manuscript Library,
         Duke University
      Sim A. DeLapp Papers
      Records and Papers of Terry Sanford

Government Documents
*Amendments to the Constitution of North Carolina, Proposed by the
   Constitutional Convention of 1875*. Raleigh: Josiah Turner, 1875.
Civil Rights Acts of 1957, 1960, 1964, 1968, and Voting Rights Act of 1965.
   Washington, D.C.: Government Printing Office, 1974.
Constitution of the State of North Carolina, 1868. Raleigh: Joseph W.
   Holden, 1868.
Eure, Thad. *Public School Laws of North Carolina*. Issued by Thad Eure,
   Secretary of State, 1955.
Final Report of the WPA Program, 1935–43. Washington, D.C.:
   Government Printing Office, 1947.
*Laws and Resolutions of the State of North Carolina, Adjourned Session
   1900*. Raleigh: Edwards and Broughton, and E. M. Uzzell, 1900.
National Emergency Council. *Report on Economic Conditions of the
   South*. [Washington, D.C.: Government Printing Office, 1938.]
President's Committee on Civil Rights. *To Secure These Rights: The*

Report of the President's Committee on Civil Rights. Washington, D.C.:
   Government Printing Office, 1947.

Public Laws of the State of North Carolina, Session of 1866. Raleigh:
   Wm. E. Pell, 1866.

Public Laws and Resolutions of the State of North Carolina, Session of 1895.
   Winston: M. I. and J. C. Stewart, 1895.

Public Laws and Resolutions of the State of North Carolina, Session of 1897.
   Winston: M. I. and J. C. Stewart, 1897.

Public Laws and Resolutions of the State of North Carolina, Session of 1899.
   Raleigh: Edwards and Broughton, and E. M. Uzzell, 1899.

Report of Population of the United States at the Eleventh Census: 1890,
   Part II. Washington, D.C.: Government Printing Office, 1897.

Revised Code of North Carolina, 1854. Boston: Little, Brown, and
   Company, 1855.

Session Laws and Resolutions, State of North Carolina, 1955. Winston-
   Salem: Winston Printing Company, 1955.

*Session Laws and Resolutions, State of North Carolina, Extra Session of
   1956, and Regular Session, 1957.* Winston-Salem: Winston Printing
   Company, 1957.

Session Laws of the State of North Carolina, Regular Session, 1965.
   Winston-Salem: Winston Printing Company, n.d.

Session Laws and Resolutions, State of North Carolina, Extra Session, 1965.
   Winston-Salem: Winston Printing Company, n.d.

Session Laws and Resolutions, State of North Carolina, Extra Session, 1966.
   Winston-Salem: Winston Printing Company, n.d.

*Session Laws and Resolutions, State of North Carolina, Regular Session,
   1967.* Winston-Salem: Winston Printing Company, n.d.

*Session Laws and Resolutions, State of North Carolina, Regular Session,
   1971.* Winston-Salem: Winston Printing Company, 1971.

*Statutes at Large, Treaties, and Proclamations of the United States of
   America from December 1865 to March 1867.* Boston: Little, Brown,
   and Company, 1868.

*Tenth Annual Report of the Bureau of Labor Statistics of the State of North
   Carolina.* Winston: M. I. and J. C. Stewart, 1897.

Court Cases

Allison v. Sharp, 184 S.E. 27 (N.C. 1936)

Alston v. School Board of City of Norfolk, 112 F.2d 992 (4th Cir. 1940)

Baker v. Carr, 369 U.S. 186 (1962)

Bazemore v. Bertie County Board of Elections, 119 S.E.2d 637 (N.C. 1961)

Blue v. Durham Public School District, 95 F. Supp. 441 (M.D.N.C. 1951)

Brown v. Board of Education of Topeka, 347 U.S. 483 (1954)

Brown v. Board of Education of Topeka, 349 U.S. 294 (1955)

Citizens United v. Federal Election Commission, 558 U.S. 310 (2010)

Drum v. Seawell, 249 F. Supp. 877 (M.D.N.C. 1965)

Dunston v. Scott, 336 F. Supp. 206 (E.D.N.C. 1972)

Gantt v. Clemson Agricultural College of South Carolina, 320 F.2d 611 (4th
  Cir. 1963)

Gingles v. Edmisten, 590 F. Supp. 345 (E.D.N.C. 1984)

Holmes v. Moore, COA19-762 (Feb. 18, 2020)

Lassiter v. Northampton County Board of Elections, 102 S.E.2d 853 (N.C.
  1958)

Lassiter v. Northampton County Board of Elections, 360 U.S. 45 (1959)

Lassiter v. Taylor, 152 F. Supp. 295 (E.D.N.C. 1957)

North Carolina State Conference of the NAACP v. Cooper, 1:18CV1034
  (M.D.N.C. Dec. 31, 2019)

North Carolina State Conference of the NAACP v. McCrory, Civ. No. 1:13-
  cv-658, Aug. 12, 2013

North Carolina State Conference of the NAACP v. McCrory, 182 F. Supp.
  3d 320 (M.D.N.C. 2016)

North Carolina State Conference of the NAACP v. McCrory, No. 16-1468
  (4th Cir. 2016)

North Carolina v. North Carolina State Conference of the NAACP, 137
  S. Ct. 1399 (2017)

Reynolds v. Sims, 377 U.S. 533 (1964)

Speechnow.org v. FEC, No. 08-5223 (D.C. Cir. 2010)

United States v. North Carolina, 1:13CV861 (M.D.N.C. Feb. 6, 2014)

Walker v. Moss, 97 S.E.2d 836 (N.C. 1957)

Watkins v. City of Wilson, 121 S.E.2d 861 (N.C. 1961)

Watkins v. Wilson, 370 U.S. 46 (1962)

Wesberry v. Sanders, 376 U.S. 1 (1964)

Newspapers

Atlanta Daily World

Carolina Times (Durham, N.C.)

Caucasian (Clinton, N.C.)

Charlotte Daily Observer

Charlotte Observer

Chicago Defender

Congressional Record

Enquirer (Tarboro, N.C.)

Greensboro (N.C.) Daily News

Greensboro (N.C.) Patriot

Indianapolis Recorder

Morning Post (Raleigh, N.C.)

Morning Star (Wilmington, N.C.)

News and Observer (Raleigh, N.C.)

New York Times

Norfolk Journal and Guide

Old North State (Salisbury, N.C.)

Pittsburgh Courier

Public Ledger (Oxford, N.C.)
Semi-weekly Standard
   (Raleigh, N.C.)
Southern Textile Bulletin
Triad Business Journal
Union Herald (Raleigh, N.C.)

Union Republican (Winston, N.C.)
Washington Post
Wilmington (N.C.) Journal
Wilmington (N.C.) Messenger
Winston-Salem (N.C.) Journal

Books, Articles, Pamphlets, and Theses

Abrams, Douglas Carl. *Conservative Constraints: North Carolina and the New Deal.* Jackson: University Press of Mississippi, 1992.

Anderson, Carol. *One Person, No Vote: How Voter Suppression Is Destroying Our Democracy.* New York: Bloomsbury, 2018.

———. *White Rage: The Unspoken Truth of Our Racial Divide.* New York: Bloomsbury, 2016.

Anderson, Eric. *Race and Politics in North Carolina, 1872–1901: The "Black Second" Congressional District.* Baton Rouge: Louisiana University Press, 1978.

Andrews, Sidney. *The South since the War, as Shown by Fourteen Weeks of Travel and Observation in Georgia and the Carolinas.* Boston: Ticknor and Fields, 1866.

Ashby, Warren. *Frank Porter Graham, a Southern Liberal.* Winston-Salem: J. F. Blair, 1980.

Ashmore, Harry S. *Civil Rights and Wrongs: A Memoir of Race and Politics, 1944–1996.* Columbia: University of South Carolina Press, 1997.

Badger, Anthony J. *North Carolina and the New Deal.* Raleigh: North Carolina Department of Cultural Resources, Division of Archives and History, 1981.

Barber, William J., II. *The Third Reconstruction: Moral Mondays, Fusion Politics, and the Rise of a New Justice Movement.* Boston: Beacon, 2016.

Barksdale, Marcellus Chandler. "The Indigenous Civil Rights Movement and Cultural Change in North Carolina: Weldon, Chapel Hill, and Monroe, 1946–1965." PhD diss., Duke University, 1977.

Batchelor, John E. *Race and Education in North Carolina: From Segregation to Desegregation.* Baton Rouge: Louisiana State University Press, 2015.

Beckel, Deborah. *Radical Reform: Interracial Politics in Post-Emancipation North Carolina.* Charlottesville: University of Virginia Press, 2011.

Berman, Ari. *Give Us the Ballot: The Modern Struggle for Voting Rights in America.* New York: Farrar, Straus and Giroux, 2015.

Bernstein, Leonard. "The Participation of Negro Delegates in the

Constitutional Convention of 1868 in North Carolina." *Journal of Negro History* 34 (October 1949): 391–409.

Brisson, Jim D. "'Civil Government Was Crumbling around Me': The Kirk-Holden War of 1870." *North Carolina Historical Review* 88 (April 2011): 123–63.

Brown, Leslie. *Upbuilding Black Durham: Gender, Class, and Black Community Development in the Jim Crow South.* Chapel Hill: University of North Carolina Press, 2008.

Browning, James B. "The North Carolina Black Code." *Journal of Negro History* 15 (October 1930): 461–73.

Campbell, Karl E. *Senator Sam Ervin, Last of the Founding Fathers.* Chapel Hill: University of North Carolina Press, 2007.

Cannon, Lou. *President Reagan: The Role of a Lifetime.* New York: Simon and Schuster 1991.

Carmichael, Orton H. *Lincoln's Gettysburg Address.* New York: Abingdon Press, 1917.

Carter, Dan T. *The Politics of Rage: George Wallace, the Origins of the New Conservatism, and the Transformation of American Politics.* New York: Simon and Schuster, 1995.

Chafe, William H. *Civilities and Civil Rights: Greensboro, North Carolina, and the Black Struggle for Freedom.* New York: Oxford University Press, 1980.

Christensen, Rob. *The Paradox of Tar Heel Politics: The Personalities, Elections, and Events That Shaped Modern North Carolina.* Chapel Hill: University of North Carolina Press, 2008.

———. *The Rise and Fall of the Branchhead Boys: North Carolina's Scott Family and the Era of Progressive Politics.* Chapel Hill: University of North Carolina Press, 2019.

Clendenen, Clarence C. "President Hayes' 'Withdrawal' of the Troops: An Enduring Myth." *South Carolina Historical Magazine* 70 (October 1969): 240–50.

Combs, Barbara Harris. *From Selma to Montgomery: The Long March to Freedom.* New York: Routledge, 2014.

Connor, R. D. W., and Clarence H. Poe, eds. *The Life and Speeches of Charles Brantley Aycock.* Garden City, N.Y.: Doubleday, Page, 1912.

Covington, Howard E., Jr., and Marion A. Ellis. *Terry Sanford: Politics, Progress, and Outrageous Ambitions.* Durham, N.C.: Duke University Press, 1999.

Crow, Jeffrey J. "Cracking the Solid South: Populism and the Fusionist Interlude." In *The North Carolina Experience: An Interpretive and*

Documentary History, edited by Lindley S. Butler and Alan D. Watson, 333–54. Chapel Hill: University of North Carolina Press, 1984.

Culver, John C., and John Hyde. *American Dreamer: A Life of Henry A. Wallace*. New York: W. W. Norton, 2000.

Dalfiume, Richard M. "The 'Forgotten Years' of the Negro Revolution." *Journal of American History* 55 (June 1968): 90–106.

Devine, Thomas W. *Henry Wallace's 1948 Presidential Campaign and the Future of Postwar Liberalism*. Chapel Hill: University of North Carolina Press, 2013.

Douglas, Davison M. *Reading, Writing, and Race: The Desegregation of the Charlotte Schools*. Chapel Hill: University of North Carolina Press, 1995.

Drescher, John. *Triumph of Good Will: How Terry Sanford Beat a Champion of Segregation and Reshaped the South*. Jackson: University Press of Mississippi, 2000.

Du Bois, W. E. Burghardt. *Black Reconstruction in America: An Essay toward a History of the Part Which Black Folk Played in the Attempt to Reconstruct Democracy in America, 1860–1880*. New York: Harcourt, Brace, and Company, 1935.

Durrill, Wayne K. "Producing Poverty: Local Government and Economic Development in a New South County, 1874–1884." *Journal of American History* 71 (March 1985): 764–81.

———. *War of Another Kind: A Southern Community in the Great Rebellion*. New York: Oxford University Press, 1990.

Earls, Anita S., Emily Wynes, and LeeAnne Quatrucci. "Voting Rights in North Carolina, 1982–2006." *Southern California Review of Law and Social Justice* 17, no. 2 (2008): 577–642.

Edmonds, Helen G. *The Negro and Fusion Politics in North Carolina, 1894–1901*. Chapel Hill: University of North Carolina Press, 1951.

Escott, Paul D. *Many Excellent People: Power and Privilege in North Carolina, 1850–1900*. Chapel Hill: University of North Carolina Press, 1985.

Esty, Amos. "North Carolina Republicans and the Conservative Revolution, 1964–1968." *North Carolina Historical Review* 82 (January 2005): 1–32.

Faulkenbury, Evan. *Poll Power: The Voter Education Project and the Movement for the Ballot in the American South*. Chapel Hill: University of North Carolina Press, 2019.

Foner, Eric. *Reconstruction: America's Unfinished Revolution, 1863–1877*. New York: Harper and Row, 1988.

————. *The Second Founding: How the Civil War and Reconstruction Remade the Constitution*. New York: W. W. Norton, 2019.

Garcia, George F. "Black Disaffection from the Republican Party During the Presidency of Herbert Hoover, 1928–1932." *Annals of Iowa* 45, no. 6 (1980): 462–77.

Gershenhorn, Jerry. "A Courageous Voice for Black Freedom: Louis Austin and the *Carolina Times* in Depression-Era North Carolina." *North Carolina Historical Review* 87 (January 2010): 57–92.

————. *Louis Austin and the* Carolina Times: *A Life in the Long Black Freedom Struggle*. Chapel Hill: University of North Carolina Press, 2018.

Gilmore, Glenda Elizabeth. *Gender and Jim Crow: Women and the Politics of White Supremacy in North Carolina, 1896–1920*. Chapel Hill: University of North Carolina Press, 1996.

Goldfield, David. *Still Fighting the Civil War: The American South and Southern History*. Baton Rouge: Louisiana State University Press, 2002.

Goldstein, Jared A. "The American Liberty League and the Rise of Constitutional Nationalism." *Temple Law Review* 86 (Winter 2014): 287–330.

The Good Health Campaign of North Carolina. N.p.: n.p., 1947.

Graf, Leroy P., and Ralph W. Haskins, eds. *The Papers of Andrew Johnson*. Vol. 6, *1862–1864*. Knoxville: University of Tennessee Press, 1983.

Gregory, James N. "The Second Great Migration: A Historical Overview." In *African American Urban History: The Dynamics of Race, Class, and Gender since World War II*, edited by Kenneth L. Kusmer and Joe W. Trotter Jr., 19–38. Chicago: University of Chicago Press, 2009.

Grosso, Catherine M., and Barbara O'Brien. "A Stubborn Legacy: The Overwhelming Importance of Race in Jury Selection in 173 Post-Batson North Carolina Capital Trials." *Iowa Law Review* 97 (July 2012): 1531–59.

Hall, Jacquelyn Dowd, James Leloudis, Robert Korstad, Mary Murphy, Lu Ann Jones, and Christopher B. Daly. *Like a Family: The Making of a Southern Cotton Mill World*. Chapel Hill: University of North Carolina Press, 1987.

Hamilton, Joseph Grégoire de Roulhac, ed. *Papers of Randolph Abbott Shotwell*. Vol. 2. Raleigh: North Carolina Historical Commission, 1931.

————. *The Papers of Thomas Ruffin*. Vol. 3. Raleigh: Edwards and Broughton, 1920.

————. *Reconstruction in North Carolina*. New York: Columbia University, 1914.

Hanchett, Thomas W. *Sorting Out the New South City: Race, Class, and Urban Development in Charlotte, 1875–1975*. Chapel Hill: University of North Carolina Press, 1998.

Heberlig, Eric S., Peter L. Francia, and Steven H. Greene. "The Conditional Party Teams of the 2008 North Carolina Federal Elections." In *The Change Election: Money, Mobilization, and Persuasion in the 2008 Federal Elections*, edited by David B. Magleby, 108–39. Philadelphia: Temple University Press, 2011.

Helper, Hinton Rowan. *The Impending Crisis of the South: How to Meet It*. New York: Burdick Brothers, 1857.

Herbin-Triant, Elizabeth A. "Southern Segregation South Africa–Style: Maurice Evans, Clarence Poe, and the Ideology of Rural Segregation." *Agricultural History* 87 (Spring 2013): 170–93.

Herron, Michael C., and Daniel A. Smith. "Race, *Shelby County*, and the Voter Information Verification Act in North Carolina." *Florida State University Law Review* 43, no. 2 (Winter 2016): 465–506.

Jeffrey, Thomas E. "'Free Suffrage' Revisited: Party Politics and Constitutional Reform in Antebellum North Carolina." *North Carolina Historical Review* 59 (January 1982): 24–48.

Jenkins, Philip. *Hoods and Shirts: The Extreme Right in Pennsylvania, 1925–1950*. Chapel Hill: University of North Carolina Press, 1997.

Johnson, Guy B. "Does the South Owe the Negro a New Deal?" *Social Forces* 13 (October 1934): 100–103.

Jones, William P. *The March on Washington: Jobs, Freedom, and the Forgotten History of Civil Rights*. New York: W. W. Norton, 2013.

Justesen, Benjamin R. *George Henry White: An Even Chance in the Race of Life*. Baton Rouge: Louisiana State University Press, 2001.

Katznelson, Ira. *Fear Itself: The New Deal and the Origins of Our Time*. New York: Liveright, 2013.

Keech, William R., and Michael P. Sistrom. *Implementation of the Voting Rights Act in North Carolina*. Pasadena: Division of the Humanities and Social Sciences, California Institute of Technology, 1992.

Kellam, James Patrick. "Helms, Hunt, and Whiteness: The 1984 Senate Campaign in North Carolina." MA thesis, Appalachian State University, 2017.

Key, V. O., Jr. *Southern Politics in State and Nation*. Knoxville: University of Tennessee Press, 1984.

Keyssar, Alexander. *The Right to Vote: The Contested History of Democracy in the United States*. Rev. ed. New York: Basic Books, 2009.

Korstad, Robert Rodgers. *Civil Rights Unionism: Tobacco Workers and the*

Struggle for Democracy in the Mid-Twentieth-Century South. Chapel Hill: University of North Carolina Press, 2003.

Korstad, Robert R., and James L. Leloudis. *To Right These Wrongs: The North Carolina Fund and the Battle to End Poverty and Inequality in 1960s America*. Chapel Hill: University of North Carolina Press, 2010.

Kotch, Seth, and Robert P. Mosteller. "The Racial Justice Act and the Long Struggle with Race and the Death Penalty in North Carolina." *North Carolina Law Review* 88, no. 6 (2010): 2031–2131.

Kousser, J. Morgan. *Colorblind Injustice: Minority Voting Rights and the Undoing of the Second Reconstruction*. Chapel Hill: University of North Carolina Press, 1999.

———. "Progressivism—for Middle-Class Whites Only: North Carolina Education, 1880–1910." *Journal of Southern History* 46 (May 1980): 169–94.

———. *The Shaping of Southern Politics: Suffrage Restriction and the Establishment of the One-Party South*. New Haven, Conn.: Yale University Press, 1974.

Ladd, Everett Carll, Jr., with Charles D. Hadley. *Transformations of the American Party System: Political Coalitions from the New Deal to the 1970s*. New York: W. W. Norton, 1975.

Laney, Garrine P. *The Voting Rights Act of 1965: Historical Background and Current Issues*. Hauppauge, N.Y.: Novinka Books, 2003.

Larkins, John R. *The Negro Population of North Carolina: Social and Economic*. Raleigh: North Carolina State Board of Charities and Public Welfare, 1944.

Lawson, Steven F. *Black Ballots: Voting Rights in the South, 1944–1969*. New York: Columbia University Press, 1976.

Lawson, William H. *No Small Thing: The 1963 Mississippi Freedom Vote*. Oxford: University Press of Mississippi, 2018.

Lewis, Sinclair. *Cheap and Contented Labor: The Picture of a Southern Mill Town in 1929*. New York: United Features Syndicate, 1929.

Lichtman, Allan J. *The Embattled Vote in America: From the Founding to the Present*. Cambridge, Mass.: Harvard University Press, 2018.

Link, William A. *Righteous Warrior: Jesse Helms and the Rise of Modern Conservatism*. New York: St. Martin's Press, 2008.

Manderson, Marge. "Review of the Patterns and Practices of Racial Discrimination." Manuscript in authors' possession.

Martin, Charles H. "Negro Leaders, the Republican Party, and the Election of 1932." *Phylon* 32, no. 1 (1971): 85–93.

McGaughey, Ewan. *A Casebook on Labour Law*. Oxford: Hart Publishing, 2019.

McKinney, Charles W., Jr. *Greater Freedom: The Evolution of the Civil Rights Struggle in Wilson, North Carolina*. Lanham, Md.: University Press of America, 2010.

Milkis, Sidney M. "The New Deal, the Decline of Parties and the Administrative State." PhD diss., University of Pennsylvania, 1981.

Mitchell, Memory F., ed. *Messages, Addresses, and Public Papers of Terry Sanford*. Raleigh: Council of State, State of North Carolina, 1966.

Moore, John Robert. "Senator Josiah W. Bailey and the 'Conservative Manifesto' of 1937." *Journal of Southern History* 31 (February 1965): 21–39.

Moore, Nina M. *Governing Race: Policy, Process, and the Politics of Race*. Westport, Conn.: Praeger, 2000.

Morgan, Iwan. *Reagan: American Icon*. New York: Bloomsbury, 2016.

National Roster of Black Elected Officials. Washington, D.C.: Joint Center for Political Studies, 1971.

Nixon, Donna L. "The Integration of UNC-Chapel Hill—Law School First." *North Carolina Law Review* 97, no. 6 (2019): 1741–93.

North Carolina Advisory Committee to the United States Commission on Civil Rights. *Equal Protection of the Laws in North Carolina*. Washington, D.C.: Government Printing Office, 1962.

———. "Voting and Voter Registration in North Carolina, 1960." Bound typescript report, North Carolina Collection, Wilson Library, University of North Carolina at Chapel Hill.

O'Connor, Paul T. "Reapportionment and Redistricting: Redrawing the Political Landscape." *North Carolina Insight* (December 1990): 30–49.

Okun, Tema. *The Emperor Has No Clothes: Teaching about Race and Racism to People Who Don't Want to Know*. Charlotte: Information Age, 2010.

Orth, John V. "North Carolina Constitutional History." *North Carolina Law Review* 70 (1991–92): 1759–1802.

Owens, Susie Lee. "The Union League of America: Political Activities in Tennessee, the Carolinas, and Virginia, 1865–1870." PhD diss., New York University, 1943.

Patterson, James T. "The Failure of Party Realignment in the South, 1937–1939." *Journal of Politics* 27 (August 1965): 602–17.

Patton, Patrick C. "Standing at Thermopylae: A History of the American Liberty League." PhD diss., Temple University, 2015.

Pearce, Gary. *Jim Hunt: A Biography*. Winston-Salem, N.C.: John F. Blair, 2010.

Perlstein, Rick. *Nixonland: The Rise of a President and the Fracturing of America*. New York: Scribner, 2008.

"Personal Profile: Edwin Pate." *Journal of Agricultural and Food Chemistry* 4 (November 1956): 975.

Petty, Adrienne Monteith. *Standing Their Ground: Small Farmers in North Carolina since the Civil War*. New York: Oxford University Press, 2013.

Phillips, Kevin P. *The Emerging Republican Majority*. Princeton, N.J.: Princeton University Press, 2015.

Pleasants, Julian M., and Augustus M. Burns III. *Frank Porter Graham and the 1950 Senate Race in North Carolina*. Chapel Hill: University of North Carolina Press, 1990.

Powell, William S., ed. *Dictionary of North Carolina Biography*. Vol. 3, *H–K*. Chapel Hill: University of North Carolina Press, 1988.

Prather, H. Leon, Sr. "The Red Shirt Movement in North Carolina, 1898–1900." *Journal of Negro History* 62 (April 1977): 174–84.

Proceedings of the Colored National Labor Convention Held in Washington, D.C., December 6th, 7th, 8th, 9th, and 10th, 1869. Washington, D.C.: New Era, 1870.

Prominent People of North Carolina: Brief Biographies of Leading People for Ready Reference Purposes. Asheville, N.C.: Evening News Publishing Company, 1906.

Raper, Horace W. *William W. Holden: North Carolina's Political Enigma*. Chapel Hill: University of North Carolina Press, 1985.

Redding, Kent. *Making Race, Making Power: North Carolina's Road to Disfranchisement*. Urbana: University of Illinois Press, 2003.

Robin, Corey. *The Reactionary Mind: Conservatism from Edmund Burke to Donald Trump*. New York: Oxford University Press, 2018.

Roth, Zachary. *The Great Suppression: Voting Rights, Corporate Cash, and the Conservative Assault on Democracy*. New York: Crown, 2016.

Schreiber, E. M. "'Where the Ducks Are': Southern Strategy versus Fourth Party." *Public Opinion Quarterly* 35 (Summer 1971): 157–67.

Shin, Eui Hang. "Black-White Differentials in Infant Mortality in the South, 1940–1970." *Demography* 12 (February 1975): 1–19.

Sitkoff, Harvard. *Toward Freedom Land: The Long Struggle for Racial Equality in America*. Lexington: University Press of Kentucky, 2010.

Snider, William D. *Helms and Hunt: The North Carolina Senate Race, 1984*. Chapel Hill: University of North Carolina Press, 1985.

Stedman, A. J. *Murder and Mystery: History of the Life and Death of John W. Stephens, State Senator of North Carolina, from Caswell County*. Greensboro, N.C.: Patriot Print, 1870.

Thuesen, Sarah C. *Greater Than Equal: African American Struggles for*

Schools and Citizenship in North Carolina, 1919–1965. Chapel Hill: University of North Carolina Press, 2013.

Towe, William H. *Barriers to Black Political Participation in North Carolina*. Atlanta: Voter Education Project, 1972.

Trelease, Allen W. "The Fusion Legislatures of 1895 and 1897: A Roll-Call Analysis of the North Carolina House of Representatives." *North Carolina Historical Review* 57 (July 1980): 280–309.

Troxler, Carole Watterson. "'To Look More Closely at the Man': Wyatt Outlaw, a Nexus of National, Local, and Personal History." *North Carolina Historical Review* 77 (October 2000): 403–33.

Uesugi, Sayoko. "Gender, Race, and the Cold War: Mary Price and the Progressive Party in North Carolina, 1945–1948." *North Carolina Historical Review* 77 (July 2000): 269–311.

Umfleet, LeRae Sikes. *A Day of Blood: The 1898 Wilmington Race Riot*. Chapel Hill: University of North Carolina Press, 2009.

Waldman, Michael. *The Fight to Vote*. New York: Simon and Schuster, 2016.

Ward, Jason Morgan. *Defending White Democracy: The Making of a Segregationist Movement and the Remaking of Racial Politics, 1936–1965*. Chapel Hill: University of North Carolina Press, 2011.

Watson, Harry L. "North Carolina Redistricting Process, 1965–1966." Manuscript in authors' possession.

Wertheimer, John W. *Law and Society in the South: A History of North Carolina Court Cases*. Lexington: University Press of Kentucky, 2009.

Wettach, Robert H. "North Carolina School Legislation, 1956." *North Carolina Law Review* 35, no. 1 (1956): 1–16.

Whalan, Mark. *The Great War and the Culture of the New Negro*. Gainesville: University Press of Florida, 2008.

Williams, Chad L. *Torchbearers of Democracy: African American Soldiers in the World War I Era*. Chapel Hill: University of North Carolina Press, 2010.

Williamson, Joel. *Crucible of Race: Black-White Relations in the American South since Emancipation*. New York: Oxford University Press, 1984.

Winford, Brandon K. *John Hervey Wheeler, Black Banking, and the Economic Struggle for Civil Rights*. Lexington: University Press of Kentucky, 2020.

Winquist, Thomas R. "Civil Rights: Legislation: The Civil Rights Act of 1957." *Michigan Law Review* 56 (February 1958): 619–30.

Woodward, C. Vann. *Origins of the New South, 1877–1913*. Baton Rouge: Louisiana University Press, 1971.

———. *Reunion and Reaction: The Compromise of 1877 and the End of Reconstruction*. Boston: Little, Brown, 1966.

Wright, Gavin. *Old South, New South: Revolutions in the Southern Economy since the Civil War*. New York: Basic Books, 1986.

Yearns, W. Buck, and John G. Barrett, eds. *North Carolina Civil War Documentary*. Chapel Hill: University of North Carolina Press, 1980.

Zieger, Robert. *The CIO: 1935–1955*. Chapel Hill: University of North Carolina Press, 1995.

Zogry, Kenneth Joel. "The House That Dr. Pope Built: Race, Politics, Memory, and the Early Struggle for Civil Rights in North Carolina." PhD diss., University of North Carolina, 2008.

Online Sources

All online sources were last accessed on February 20, 2020.

1898 Wilmington Race Riot Report. 1898 Wilmington Race Riot Commission, May 31, 2006. http://bit.ly/2HOWsgJ.

"1964 Presidential General Election Results—North Carolina." *Dave Leip's Atlas of U.S. Presidential Elections*. http://bit.ly/34aL7Aa.

"1968 Presidential General Election Results—North Carolina." *Dave Leip's Atlas of U.S. Presidential Elections*. http://bit.ly/2LMlhvX.

"2008 Democratic Party Platform." *American Presidency Project*. http://bit.ly/2ti7IhI.

"2013–14 School Performance Grades (A–F) for North Carolina Public Schools." North Carolina Department of Public Instruction, February 5, 2015. http://bit.ly/2Ruw7Ki.

"2013–2015 North Carolina Budget Short-Changes Students, Teachers, and Public Education." Budget and Tax Center, North Carolina Justice Center, August 2013. http://bit.ly/2RTBUrA.

"2019 Annual Report." Civitas Institute. http://bit.ly/36Bpzhf.

An Act to Amend the North Carolina Constitution to Require Photo Identification to Vote in Person, S.L. 2018-128, House Bill 1092. http://bit.ly/2LRAE5p.

Alsop, Stewart. "Can Goldwater Win in 64?" *Saturday Evening Post*, August 24, 1963. http://bit.ly/2ScogwW.

American Express Merchant Reference Guide—U.S. https://amex.co/2HKPqtq.

"America the Vulnerable: The Problem of Duplicate Voting." Government Accountability Institute. http://bit.ly/2uFgVRA.

"Anti-Heagarty Ads: We Just Threw Up in Our Mouths." *Indy Week*, November 1, 2010. http://bit.ly/2tmNfZ3.

Atkeson, Lonna Rae, Lisa A. Bryant, Thad E. Hall, Kyle L. Saunders, and R. Michael Alvarez. "New Barriers to Participation: Application of New Mexico's Voter Identification Law." Caltech/MIT Voting Technology Project. http://bit.ly/2LSocT6.

Bailey, Kristy. "Gaps in Voter Registration Process Raise Concerns of Fraud." *Carolina Journal*, October 26, 2010. http://bit.ly/2UjDAxs.

Blake, John. "What Black America Won't Miss about Obama." *CNN*, July 1, 2016. https://cnn.it/2tXfX2E.

Blest, Paul. "Over 80,000 People Joined the Biggest-Ever Moral March in North Carolina." *Nation*, February 13, 2017. http://bit.ly/2ROVZAw.

Boughton, Melissa. "N.C. Court of Appeals Throws Out Voter Photo I.D. for Now, Says Law Likely Passed with Discriminatory Intent." N.C. Policy Watch, February 18, 2020. http://bit.ly/2Lsgzms.

Brenneman, Ross. "Teacher Attrition Continues to Plague North Carolina." *Education Week*, October 13, 2015. http://bit.ly/2uuLBVu.

"Brief of Harry McMullan, Attorney General of North Carolina, Amicus Curiae." *Brown v. Board of Education*, 349 U.S. 294 (1955). Gale, *The Making of Modern Law, U.S. Supreme Court Records and Briefs, 1832–1978*. http://bit.ly/36PHJfd.

Broockman, David, and Ethan Roeder. "Hispanics Are the Future of Progressive Strength in America." New Organizing Institute. http://bit.ly/2HPJ3Fn.

Butterfield, George Kenneth Jr. Interview, Behind the Veil: Documenting African-American Life in the Jim Crow South Digital Collection. John Hope Franklin Research Center, Duke University Libraries. http://bit.ly/2RMrziw.

Charlotte-Mecklenburg Board of Education. Meeting minutes, September 8, 2009. http://bit.ly/2LQCjYX.

"The Circus Goes On." Civitas Institute, October 8, 2013. http://bit.ly/2GuzPoc.

"Citizens without Proof: A Survey of Americans' Possession of Documentary Proof of Citizenship and Photo Identification." Brennan Center for Justice. http://bit.ly/34QpHtJ.

Coates, Ta-Nehisi. "The Case for Reparations." *Atlantic*, June 2014. http://bit.ly/2NtghNz.

Collins, William J., and Robert A. Margo. "Historical Perspectives on Racial Differences in Schooling in the United States." Working Paper No. 03-W13, Department of Economics, Vanderbilt University, June 2003. http://bit.ly/2UMbN7e.

Dickman, Sam, David Himmelstein, Danny McCormick, and Steffie Woolhandler. "Opting Out of Medicaid Expansion: The Health and

Financial Impacts." *Health Affairs*, January 30, 2014. http://bit.ly
/36vsOa4.

"Easley Testifies to State Board of Elections." Video, *WRAL.com*, October
29, 2009. http://bit.ly/2UAWq1h.

Florsheim, Lane. "Four Inmates Might Return to Death Row Because
North Carolina Repealed a Racial Justice Law." *New Republic*, May 9,
2014. http://bit.ly/37qiEss.

Forest, Dan. Twitter posts. December 27, 2019, http://bit.ly/2IOFlM3,
and February 18, 2020, http//: bit.ly/2XoEMiU.

Gantt, Harvey B. Interview C-0008. Southern Oral History Program
Collection #4007, Documenting the American South, University of
North Carolina Libraries. https://unc.live/31hWV3N.

Garfield, Rachel, and Anthony Damico. "The Coverage Gap: Uninsured
Poor Adults in States That Do Not Expand Medicaid—an Update."
Henry J. Kaiser Family Foundation, January 2016. http://bit.ly
/30PNZlX.

Gerhardt, Deborah R. "Pay Our Teachers or Lose Your Job." *Slate*,
January 5, 2014. http://bit.ly/2ROO19t.

Gitterman, Daniel P., Peter A. Coclanis, and John Quinterno. "Recession
and Recovery in North Carolina: A Data Snapshot, 2007–12." August
12, 2012, Global Research Institute, University of North Carolina at
Chapel Hill. https://unc.live/2HSb8vw.

Goldenberg, Richard. "African-American Troops Fought to Fight in World
War I." *U.S. Department of Defense—News*. http://bit.ly/2RGDBKo.

Goldsmith, Thomas. "Thomas Farr, Jesse Helms, and the Return of the
Segregationists." *Indy Week*, January 3, 2018. http://bit.ly/36QLq4c.

"GOP Featured McCollum in 2010 Attack Ad." *WRAL.com*, September 4,
2014. http://bit.ly/37SalWG.

"GOP Mailing Depicts Obama on Food Stamps, Not Dollar Bill." *NPR*,
October 16, 2008. https://n.pr/34GHrHT.

Griffin, Lloyd E. Interview C-0135, Southern Oral History Program
Collection #4007, Documenting the American South, University of
North Carolina Libraries. https://unc.live/2sJqY7p.

"'Hanging Obama' Truck Makes Way into Charlotte." *WBTV*,
September 6, 2012. http://bit.ly/32sZJu4.

Helms, Jesse. Hands ad. http://bit.ly/2Q5zJnr.

House Bill 589. General Assembly of North Carolina, Session 2013.
http://bit.ly/2Sot64K.

"Immigration Is Changing the Political Landscape in Key States." Center
for American Progress. https://ampr.gs/32wwPsW.

Johnson, Cedric D., and Matthew Ellinwood. *Smart Money: Investing in*

Student Achievement. North Carolina Justice Center. http://bit.ly/37tcCqO.

Johnson, Lyndon B. "President Johnson's Special Message to the Congress: The American Promise." LBJ Presidential Library. http://bit.ly/38toWIK.

Joint Resolution Acknowledging the Findings of the 1898 Wilmington Race Riot Commission, General Assembly of North Carolina, 2007-67, August 2, 2007. http://bit.ly/2Nr2tTJ.

Kornegay, Horace. Interview C-0165. Southern Oral History Program Collection #4007, Documenting the American South, University of North Carolina Libraries. https://unc.live/2OlHGBr.

Kromm, Chris. "Art Pope Bankrolls Dubious 'Voter Fraud' Crusade." *Facing South*, October 28, 2010. http://bit.ly/36JMKpC.

———. "Art Pope's Big Day: Republican Benefactor Fueled GOP Capture of N.C. Legislature." *Facing South*, November 9, 2010. http://bit.ly/37PoDUZ.

Ku, Leighton, Brian Bruen, Erika Steinmetz, and Tyler Bysshe. *The Economic and Employment Costs of Not Expanding Medicaid in North Carolina: A County-Level Analysis*. Cone Health Foundation and Kate B. Reynolds Charitable Trust. http://bit.ly/30TMfI5.

Ladd, Helen F., Charles T. Clotfelter, and John B. Holbein. "The Growing Segmentation of the Charter School Sector in North Carolina." National Bureau of Economic Research, April 2015. http://bit.ly/36P2cRw.

"Latinos in the 2016 Election: North Carolina." Pew Research Center. https://pewrsr.ch/2HOyFNV.

Levitt, Justin. "The Truth about Voter Fraud." Brennan Center for Justice, New York University School of Law. http://bit.ly/2Nj7IVk.

"The Madison Project Launches the Code Red USA Project." Madison Project, August 24, 2012. http://bit.ly/2UHlrrE.

Mastercard Transaction Processing Rules. http://bit.ly/32w1iaI.

Mayer, Jane. "Covert Operations." *New Yorker*, August 23, 2010. http://bit.ly/30m6w8Z.

———. "State for Sale: A Conservative Multimillionaire Has Taken Control in North Carolina, One of 2012's Top Battlegrounds." *New Yorker*, October 13, 2011. http://bit.ly/37VMm96.

Millhiser, Ian. "The Cracks in the GOP's Gerrymandering Firewall." *Vox*, September 11, 2019. http://bit.ly/35Tq1qL.

Mitchell, Tazra. "North Carolina's Earned Income Tax Credit." *BTC Brief*, Budget and Tax Center, North Carolina Justice Center, February 2013. http://bit.ly/2RrzrpA.

Mixon, Jeff. "Just Look at the Results." *Red Clay Citizen*, March 27, 2009. http://bit.ly/32tZmj1.

———. "Narco Gangs in North Carolina." *Civitas Review Online*, April 1, 2009. http://bit.ly/2HNmPnq.

———. "Who Benefits from Illegal Immigration?" *Civitas Review Online*, October 14, 2009. http://bit.ly/2I3fLTV.

"NCAE Wins Challenge to Payroll Dues Ban." *WRAL.com*, January 3, 2013. http://bit.ly/36pN1xK.

"NCGOP Sees Encouraging Early Voting, Obama/Clinton Coalition Tired, Fail to Resonate in North Carolina." North Carolina Republican Party, November 6, 2016. http://bit.ly/2HS9B8J.

"N.C. Voter ID Law Overturned." *News and Observer* (Raleigh, N.C.), February 9, 2018. http://bit.ly/320S3cm.

Newkirk, Vann R., II. "How Redistricting Became a Technological Arms Race." *Atlantic*, October 28, 2017. http://bit.ly/2Nt5LG9.

———. "What Early Voting in North Carolina Actually Reveals." *Atlantic*, November 8, 2016. http://bit.ly/2ULBchm.

Nixon, Richard M. "Nomination Acceptance Address, August 8, 1968." *Presidential Rhetoric*. http://bit.ly/2HPCoel.

"North Carolina African-American Legislators, 1969–2019." North Carolina General Assembly, January 7, 2019. http://bit.ly/38KWFou.

"North Carolina Governor, 1892." *Our Campaigns*. http://bit.ly/320UHPk.

"North Carolina's 2013 Legislative Session Recap: Landmark Gains for Conservatism." Civitas Institute, July 30, 2013. http://bit.ly/32rgVA6.

"North Carolina's Hispanic Community: 2019 Snapshot." *Carolina Demography*. http://bit.ly/2SY8Rpd.

"North Carolina's 'Racial Justice Act.'" Civitas Institute, November 16, 2010. http://bit.ly/38K4670.

"North Carolina v. North Carolina NAACP." Moritz College of Law, Ohio State University. http://bit.ly/2W5Nd3U.

North Carolina Voter Education Project. *Know Your Voting Rights*. North Carolina Digital Collections, State Library of North Carolina. http://bit.ly/315SxVt.

———. "North Carolina Voter Education Project" (brochure). North Carolina Digital Collections, State Library of North Carolina. http://bit.ly/2Z1ZsQg.

"North Carolina Voter ID Amendment (2018)." *Ballotpedia*. http://bit.ly/32tAI1Z.

"North Carolina Voter ID Amendment Debate Features Misleading Claims." *Politifact*, November 1, 2018. http://bit.ly/32A2tpJ.

"Opportunity Scholarship Program, 2019–20 School Year," recipients by nonpublic school. North Carolina State Education Assistance Authority. http://bit.ly/2GoFFzZ.

Post-election Audit Report: General Election 2016. North Carolina State Board of Elections, April 21, 2017. http://bit.ly/2LQ3TFP.

"Private School Minority Statistics in North Carolina." Private School Review. http://bit.ly/3aJN8I4.

Public Law 85-315: An Act to Provide Means of Further Securing and Protecting the Civil Rights of Persons within the Jurisdiction of the United States (71 Stat. 634; Date: September 9, 1957; Enacted H.R. 6127). http://bit.ly/2UGEvGA.

Purdy, Jedediah. "North Carolina's Long Moral March and Its Lessons for the Trump Resistance." *New Yorker*, February 17, 2017. http://bit.ly/30k2wGk.

"Racial Resentment Adds to GOP Voter Enthusiasm." *MSNBC*, October 15, 2012. https://on.msnbc.com/2uQrSjf.

Rawls, Kristin. "The Liberal Protest That Would Shock the Right." *Salon*, July 24, 2013. http://bit.ly/3aQP41w.

Reagan, Ronald. "A Time for Choosing Address—October 27, 1964." Ronald Reagan Presidential Foundation and Institute. http://bit.ly/2RKiZRx.

Report of the North Carolina Advisory Committee on Education, April 5, 1956. http://bit.ly/2LTNQXw.

"Returning Soldiers." *Crisis* 18 (May 1919): 13–14. http://bit.ly/3b1dJ3f.

Riggs, Allison. Twitter post. February 18, 2020. http://bit.ly/33rAavk.

Riley, Nicolas. "A Lesson from North Carolina on Challenges." Brennan Center for Justice, July 2, 2012. http://bit.ly/32uhGbN.

Ross, Janell. "Number of Latino Registered Voters Doubles in North Carolina Creating Potential Long-Term Swing State." *Huffington Post—Latino Voices*, May 25, 2012. http://bit.ly/2I3lGID.

"A Sampling of Jim Crow Laws." *ANCHOR: A North Carolina History Online Resource.* http://bit.ly/2HOxXAf.

Schofield, Rob. "County-by-County Data Reveal Dramatic Impact of Proposed Election Changes on Voters." N.C. Policy Watch, July 22, 2013. http://bit.ly/2LTDMot.

School Vouchers in North Carolina: The First Three Years. Children's Law Clinic, Duke University School of Law. http://bit.ly/2Sbgo3j.

Semuels, Alana. "The Never-Ending Foreclosure." *Atlantic*, December 1, 2017. http://bit.ly/35X96mZ.

Session Law 2013-2, House Bill 4, An Act to Address the Unemployment Insurance Debt. General Assembly of North Carolina. http://bit.ly/2GnNrdE.

Sirota, Alexandra Forter. "Income Tax Rate Cap Amendment Is Costly to Taxpayers, Communities." Budget and Tax Center, North Carolina Justice Center, September 2018. http://bit.ly/3aLGJMv.

———. "Public Investment Falls, Tax Responsibility Shifts." *Altered State*, N.C. Policy Watch, December 2, 2015. http://bit.ly/2RsMhnh.

"State Poverty Rates by Sex and Race: 1989." U.S. Census Bureau. http://bit.ly/2Zx9lah.

Sturgis, Sue. "Art Pope–Funded Group Launches Database Targeting Moral Monday Arrestees." *Facing South*, June 19, 2013. http://bit.ly/2RwRgUc.

———. "How Art Pope Helped Turn Back the Clock on Voting Rights in North Carolina." *Facing South*, August 29, 2013. http://bit.ly/36JN5so.

"Support Voter ID Today!" Civitas Institute. http://bit.ly/33mJf8x.

"Supreme Court Ruling Brings Medicaid Expansion for N.C. into Focus." *WRAL.com*, June 25, 2015. http://bit.ly/2NX9Ank.

Tippett, Rebecca. "North Carolina Hispanics and the Electorate." *Carolina Demography*, October 9, 2014. http://bit.ly/2UDvIVC.

———. "Potential Voters Are Fastest-Growing Segment of N.C. Hispanic Population." *Carolina Demography*. http://bit.ly/2QRRpQh.

The Unraveling: Poorly-Crafted Education Policies Are Failing North Carolina's Children. Education and Law Project, North Carolina Justice Center. http://bit.ly/2TYTpcG.

Unz, Ron. "Immigration, the Republicans, and the End of White America." *American Conservative*, September 19, 2011. http://bit.ly/32sEyYY.

Visa Core Rules and Visa Product and Services Rules. https://vi.sa/2HKJGzJ.

"Voter ID: A Form of Suppression or Necessary Protection?" Civitas Institute, June 28, 2018. http://bit.ly/2IR8wOL.

"Voter ID to Go on N.C. Ballots." *Tribune Papers*, July 12, 2018. http://bit.ly/2LVTh8c.

"Voters Lower Cap on Income Taxes in North Carolina." *Governing*, November 7, 2018. http://bit.ly/2Gqro5T.

Wagner, Lindsay. "North Carolina Once Again toward the Bottom in National Rankings on Teacher Pay." N.C. Policy Watch, March 18, 2015. http://bit.ly/2TZHA67.

Wallace, Henry A. "Ten Extra Years." *Sphinx* 34 (February 1948): 12–14, 34–37. http://bit.ly/31hRDVR.

Wills, Shelda M. "Stockton, Richard Gordon." *NCPedia*, January 1, 1994. http://bit.ly/30I18xg.

Index

Page numbers in italics refer to illustrations.

Davis, Fred, Jr., 50
death penalty, 2, 102–3, *103*, 109
DeLapp, Sim A., 85–86
Democratic Party: in early 2000s,
 95; blacks turning to, 34–36, 37,
 78, 80; consolidation of power
 after 1900, 27; elections from 1877
 to 1900, 13, 15, 19–22, 24–26; and
 party label flip, 4, 88–89, 94; and
 VEP, 79; and voting rights, 22–24;
 whites turning from, 80, 84–87.
 See also specific members of
desegregation: of military, 38, 45;
 of schools, 55, 64, 66–67, 113. *See
 also* segregation
Detroit, 1967 uprising in, 87–88
Devane, W. P., 134n2
disenfranchisement, 23–24, 60
district redrawing, legislative, 1,
 83–84, 95, 104, 121. *See also* appor-
 tionment of legislative seats
Dockery, Robert W., 61
Dole, Elizabeth, 95
Double V strategy, 38
Douglas, William O., 58
Drum, Renn, Jr., 81
Drum v. Seawell, 139nn32–33
Du Bois, W. E. B., 29, 32
Dunston v. Scott, 82–83
Durham, N.C., 49, 77–78
Durham Committee on Negro Af-
 fairs, 49
Durham conference of black leaders,
 34–35

early voting, 1, 97, 101, 105–6, 116–17,
 118–19
Earned Income Tax Credit (EITC), 2,
 109–10
Easley, Michael F., 99
Eastern Council on Community Affairs, 56
eastern North Carolina counties, *xii*,
 8, 14, 52, 73, 77–78

Eaton, Rosanell, 116–17
Economic Opportunity Act, 74
Edmund Pettus Bridge, 76
education, graduate, 45, 55
education, public: charter schools
 and, 112–13; racial disparity in
 years completed, 58–59; equality
 in, 61–63; high school gradua-
 tion rates, 29, 44; Hunt and, 96;
 N.C. Constitution and, 10, 12–13;
 Pearsall Committee and, 63–64;
 reforms of 1895 and 1897 and,
 18–19; Sanford and, 69–70, *70*;
 and school performance, 29, 112;
 and segregation and desegregation of schools, 29, 55, 64, 66–67,
 113; spending on, 29, 30, 45, 90,
 111–12, *116*; teachers wages and,
 29, 60–62, 96, 112; vouchers and,
 64, 113–14
Eisenhower, Dwight D., 64
EITC (Earned Income Tax Credit), 2,
 109–10
election law reforms: Act to Regulate
 Elections, 23–24; at-large voting in
 multimember districts, 50–51, 52,
 56, 81–84; N.C. Constitution, 10,
 13, 81, 119–21; Fusion, 16–17; HB
 589, 1–2, 105–8, 114, 116–19, 122;
 literacy test and disenfranchisement, 23–24; Military Reconstruction Act of 1867, 9; Nineteenth
 Amendment to U.S. Constitution, 32–33; numbered-seat plan,
 81–82; Pearsall amendment, 64;
 photo ID requirement and, 119–
 22, *120*; single-shot voting, 51–52,
 53, *54*, 56, 63, 82–83
elections: of 1864, 7; of 1877, 13; of
 1892 and 1894, 13, 15, 129n25; of
 1896, 13, 18; of 1898, 13, 18, 19–22;
 of 1900, 13, 24–26, *25*; of 1904 and
 1912, 27; of 1936, 33–34, 35; of
 1948, 39–42, *42*; of 1950, 43–48,

Madison Project, 108
marriage, interracial, 8, 12, 28, 67
Martin, James G., 95
Mary Reynolds Babcock Foundation, 73–74
McCain, Franklin, 65
McCarthy, Joseph, 45
McCollum, Henry L., 102–3
McConnell, Mitch, 100
McCrory, Patrick L., 95, 104, 109, 115, 118
McKissick, Floyd, 55
McNeil, Joseph, 65
Mediation and Conciliation Service, federal, 38
Medicaid, 2, 110–11
Mellon, Andrew W., 44
merchants, exploitation by, 14
Michael, Leila B., 40
military desegregation, 38, 45
Military Reconstruction Act of 1867, 9, 23, 128n8
miscegenation, 8, 12, 28, 67
Mixon, Jeff, 103
Moore, Timothy K., 109, 111, 114, 119
Moral Monday movement, 2, 115–16, *116*
Morrison, Cameron, 31
mortality rates, 29–30, 131n10
multimember districts, 50–51, 52, 56, 81–84
Murray, Thomas O., 104

NAACP (National Association for the Advancement of Colored People): *Crisis* and, 32; education and teachers wages and, 60, 61, 62; Gantt and, 92; growth of, 37; HB 589 and, 2, 116–17; Sanford and, 69; SB 824 and, 121–22
National Labor Relations Board, 38
National War Labor Board, 38
NCTA (North Carolina Teachers Association), 60–62

neighborhood councils, 78
Newark, 1967 uprising in, 87–88
New Deal, 33, 35–37, 38, 44, 60
"New Negro," 33, 34
New Right, 48
News and Observer (Raleigh, N.C.), 19–20, *21*, *47*, 48, 52, *54*
New York Times, 103
Nineteenth Amendment to U.S. Constitution, 32–33
Nixon, Richard, 88
North Carolina Association of Educators, 112
North Carolina Agricultural and Technical State University. *See* Agricultural and Technical College of North Carolina
North Carolina Central University. *See* North Carolina College for Negroes
North Carolina Citizens Association, 43–44
North Carolina College for Negroes, 55
North Carolina Committee on Negro Affairs, 35
North Carolina Congressional Club, 89
North Carolina Fund, 73–75, 77–80, 87
North Carolina Independent Voters League, 35
North Carolina People's Assembly, 2
North Carolina Republican Executive Committee, 102–4, *103*, *104*
North Carolina State Conference of the NAACP v. Cooper, 145n58
North Carolina State Conference of the NAACP v. McCrory (2013), 127n2, 144n47
North Carolina State Conference of the NAACP v. McCrory (M.D.N.C. 2016), 144n48
North Carolina State Conference of

biracial, 9, 10, 15; blacks turning from, 34–35; business alignment of, 13; conservatism and, 66; executive committee, 102–4, *103*, *104*; Fusion movement and, 15, 18, 20; HB 589 and, 1–2, 108, 117–19; party label flip and, 3–4, 88–89, 94; voter photo ID requirement and, 119–21, *120*; "southern strategy" of, 85; as white man's party, 84–86, 100. *See also specific members of*

Research Triangle Park, 67

Richmond, David, 65

Riggs, Allison, 122

R. J. Reynolds Tobacco Company, 38

Reynolds v. Sims, 139n33

Roberts, John G., Jr., 118, 119

Robin, Corey, 123

Robinson, Hubert J., 135n3

Roosevelt, Eleanor, 33

Roosevelt, Franklin D., 33–34, 36, 38, 43

rural segregation, 28

Russell, Daniel L., Jr., 18

same-day voter registration, 1–2, 97, 101, 105–6, 118

Sanford, Terry, 66, 67–73, *70*, 90

Saunders, William L., 11

school desegregation, 55, 64, 66–67, 113

school performance, 29, 112

school vouchers, 64, 113–14

Schroeder, Thomas D., 117

Schwerner, Michael, 76

SCLC (Southern Christian Leadership Conference), 65, 76

Scott, W. Kerr, 41–43, 44, 48

Seabrook, James W., 62

segregation: Jim Crow and, 27–28, 30, 40, 45; Sanford and, 72, 73; schools and, 29, 55, 62–64, 66–67, 113

Senate Bill (SB) 824, 119–22, 123

separate but equal, 12–13, 55

sharecropping, 14, 55, 73

Shaw University, 65

Shelby County v. Holder, 1, 105

Simmons, Furnifold M., 19

single-shot voting, 51–52, *53*, *54*, 63, 82–83, 91, 101

sit-ins, 65, 70

slavery, abolition of, 7, 19

Sloan, Alfred P., 44

Smart Start, 96

Smith, Daniel, 105

Smith, Willis, 43, 44–48, *46–47*, *54*

SNCC (Student Nonviolent Coordinating Committee), 65, 76

Snider, William, 30

Snow, John J., Jr., 102, *103*, 104

Social Security Act of 1935, 36, 43

soldiers, black, 32

South Africa, 28

Southern Christian Leadership Conference (SCLC), 65, 76

Southern Coalition for Social Justice, 121–22

Southern Conference for Human Welfare, 43

Southern Farmers Alliance, 15

Southern Regional Council, 79

Southern Textile Bulletin, 30–31

Speechnow.org v. Federal Election Commission, 102

Stein, Joshua, 119

Stephens, John W., 11

Stevens, Thaddeus, 8–9

Stockton, Richard G., 43

straight-ticket voting, 105–6

Student Nonviolent Coordinating Committee (SNCC), 65, 76

Swann v. Charlotte-Mecklenburg Board of Education, 113

Sweatt v. Painter, 55

Tea Party, 99–100

textile industry, 14–15, 28, 29, 30, 43

Thirteenth Amendment to U.S. Constitution, 3
Thuesen, Sarah, 62
Tillis, Thom, 108
tobacco industry, 14–15, 29, 30, 38–39, *39*
To Secure These Rights report, 45
transgender people, 115
Trigg, Harold L., 43
True the Vote, 108
Truman, Harry S., 40, 45
Twentieth Century Voters Club, 32

unemployment, 2, 95, 98–99, 110
Union League, 9
unions, labor, 13, 30, 33, 37–39, 43, 60–61
United Organizations for Community Improvement (UOCI), 78
United States v. North Carolina, 142n27
Unz, Ron, 100
urban uprisings, 87–88

Vance, Zebulon B., 7, 13
Variety Wholesalers, 100–101, 102
violence, 10–12, 16, 19–22, 30, 37, 52, 55, 75–76, 87, 128n16, 130n39
Voter Education Project (VEP), 79–80
voter eligibility challenges, 17, 23, 106–8
voter fraud, 1, 101, 108, 120–21
Voter Integrity Projects, 108
voter intimidation and suppression, 16–17, 20, 24, 57, 106–8
voter participation, 97, 106, 119, 123–24
voter registration, 1–2; Act to Regulate Elections and, 23–24; blacks turning to Democratic Party and, 35, 132n23; drives for, 35, 39, 50, 79, *79*, 79–80; Fusion legislation and, 16, 17, 18; increase of in early

2000s, 97; preregistration for high schoolers and, 97, 106, 118; same-day, 1–2, 97, 101, 105–6, 118
voting rights, 1–4; campaigns for, 76; Civil Rights Act of 1964 and, 75–76; of felons, 13; Military Reconstruction Act of 1867 and, 9; N.C. Constitution and, 6, 10, 22–23, 58, 59, 61, 119–22; and preclearance provision for election law changes, 77, 82, 83, 105, 138n25; property requirements and, 6–7, 10; reforms and (*see* election law reforms); universal manhood suffrage, 10; U.S. Constitution and, 3, 22–23, 32–33, 83, 98; Voting Rights Act of 1965 and, 1, 76–77, 80, 82, 84, 85, 105, 138n25; women, 32–33
vouchers, school, 64, 113–14

Waddell, Alfred M., 22
wages: HB 2 and, 115; during Jim Crow regime, 29–30, 36, 38, 44, 60–62; teachers', 29, 60–62, 96, 112
Wagner Act, 38
Walker, James R., Jr., 55–58, *56*, 59
Walker v. Moss, 135n17
Wallace, George C., 72, 88
Wallace, Henry A., 39–41; campaign poster, *42*
war on poverty, 73, 74
Watkins, Talmadge A., 51–52
Watkins v. City of Wilson, 51–52
Watkins v. Wilson, 135n9
Watt, Mel, 84
Welch, Robert W., Jr., 86
Weldon, N.C., 55
Wesberry v. Sanders, 139n33
Wheeler, John Hervey, 71
White, George Henry, 84
White, Walter, 45
White Government Unions, 20

white supremacy: in late 1860s and 1870s, 11–13; in 1890s, 19–26; in 1950s, 52, 61, 64; Jim Crow regime and, 28–29, 30–31, 33, 34–35, 38; Racial Justice Act and, 109
Wiley, Calvin H., 7–8
Williams, Chad, 32
Williams, Kenneth R., 39
Wilmington, N.C., 20–22, 22, 130n39
Wilmington (N.C.) Journal, 11
Wilmington (N.C.) Morning Star, 22

Wilson, N.C., 35, 50–52, *51*
Wilson, Woodrow, 32
women, black, 29, 32–33, 40
Woodhouse, Dallas, 118, 121
Works Progress Administration, 33
World War I, 32, 33
World War II, 37–38, 61–62
WRAL, 45, 90

Z. Smith Reynolds Foundation, 73–74